P9-EFG-583

POPE JOHN XXIII

The Gentle Shepherd

IMMORTALS OF PHILOSOPHY AND RELIGION

POPE JOHN XXIII

The Gentle Shepherd

BY JEANETTE STRUCHEN

Illustrated with photographs

FRANKLIN WATTS, INC.
575 Lexington Avenue
New York, N.Y. 10022

5190

ACKNOWLEDGMENTS

The quotations in this book are used by permission and special arrangements with the proprietors of their respective copyrights who are listed below.

Hawthorn Books, Inc. for selection from the book A MAN NAMED JOHN, by Alden Hatch. Copyright © 1963 by Hawthorn Books, Inc. Published by Hawthorn Books, Inc., 70 Fifth Avenue, New York, New York.

McGraw-Hill Book Company for selections from JOURNAL OF A SOUL, by Pope John XXIII. © 1965 by Geoffrey Chapman Ltd. Used with permission of McGraw-Hill Book Company.

All photographs, including cover,
courtesy United Press International

*This book is dedicated to all those who,
in the spirit of
Pope John XXIII,
work to break down barriers to
Christian unity.*

CONTENTS

POPE JOHN XXIII

Man moved out of the cave by ideas.

With the same initiative he changes the course of rivers, irrigates deserts, circles the moon, and hammers out one civilization after another.

But he is forever plagued with nearsightedness and an anemic understanding of man's responsibility to man.

This book is about a man who offered vision to the nearsighted and leadership to the listless.

His leadership was two-sided. The outside framework was change. The inside was stability.

By punching holes in tradition he forced fresh air through dusty corners, renewing the old and stabilizing the new.

Such changes cannot be locked in one era. They serve as a bridge from age to age.

PROLOGUE

POPE JOHN XXIII was a priest of the Roman Catholic Church. His birth had not made headlines, and neither did his ordination. In fact, the world was scarcely aware of his presence until he was seventy-eight years old. At that time he was elected pope. The election was talked about in newscasts for several days until it gave way to fresher events. The world quietly consigned him to the mold of his papal predecessors and moved on to other interests.

But three months after his election, the world was forced to take another look. On January 26 and 27, 1959, the *Osservatore Romano* printed a short statement that Pope John had proposed a special conference to update the Church and open new channels of communication among Catholics, Protestants, and Orthodox Christians. In the next few weeks, people everywhere, in and out of the Catholic Church, began to notice the new pope. Not since the ninth century had the Orthodox religions been invited to meet, and Protestants had not convened since the sixteenth century. There was much speculation on why Pope John had made this announcement, and what it would mean.

Almost overnight a seventy-eight-year-old man had become the center of impending change. It was as though the head of a household was calling together the entire family, including the estranged cousins. Both practical and idealistic, Pope John's plan was to help the Church become a more positive influence on people. He knew that the Church must do more than preach to the world, but that it could, by inner renewal, become a loving servant to the world.

No one knew what would happen, but this idea and its results produced four of the most significant years in Catholic Church history.

On a hot July day I stood in the blistering Italian sun awaiting the appearance of Pope John XXIII in St. Peter's Square, Rome. Thousands of people had come for the Sunday noon blessing, to be given from the balcony of the pope's Vatican apartment. People had begun to arrive early, hoping for a good view of Pope John. Many carried campstools across the square, and set them down in direct line with the draped balcony. Protestants and Catholics mingled in an ever-growing crowd. Everyone kept looking from wristwatches to the balcony.

At noon double doors were flung open and Pope John XXIII, dressed in white, appeared on the balcony. Thousands of people knelt on the rough, uneven stones in the square. To some, this man was the Holy

Father, Vicar of Christ, the successor to Saint Peter himself. To others, he was a far-reaching Christian leader. To all, he was a personality with exceptional concern for universal humanity—a man who had revived the touch of the Good Shepherd in a fast-moving technical age.

Pope John spoke both in Italian and Latin. In a few minutes he turned and left the balcony, and the crowd dispersed.

What made the event special? Surely it was the presence of a man whose love and concern spread over those whom Jesus had called "the least of these my brethren."

Pope John XXIII knew about the least of the brethren. He was one of them and he lived among them.

JEANETTE STRUCHEN

POPE JOHN XXIII

The Gentle Shepherd

CHAPTER ONE

A SPECK OF GEOGRAPHY

ITALIAN VILLAGES are like small towns everywhere. They are usually identified as being a certain distance from some city or as the birthplace of an illustrious native son or daughter.

Pope John's birthplace is no exception. Sotto il Monte, in north central Italy, nestles at the foot of Monte Canto, near the city of Bergamo. In every season, Monte Canto makes itself known to the villagers below. Whether or not it is a blessing or a hazard in winter the natives do not say. The mountain is there and it reigns over the village. In return, the citizens claim proud ownership to the grandeur of it.

November 25, 1881, was a cold, wet, and windy day. During the early morning hours a child was born to Giovanni Battista and Maria Anna Mazzola Roncalli—a son who would put Sotto il Monte on the map. He was named Guiseppe Angelo (although later called Angelo Guiseppe), the fourth of the ten Roncalli children to survive infancy.

Within four hours after childbirth, Maria Roncalli

3

Pope John's parents, Maria and Giovanni Roncalli

dressed and walked several blocks in the driving rain. Then she waited four hours for a priest to baptize her baby. This says something not only about the physical stock of young Angelo's mother, but also about the importance of the Church to his family.

With rain beating against the old stucco church of San Giovanni, and the wind howling a mournful tune through the bell tower, Uncle Saverio Roncalli took the baby in his arms. Father Francesco Rebuzzini prayed the infant into the Church which would claim his devotion for some eighty years.

The Roncalli family was poor. Angelo's father was a tenant farmer on the land of Count Ottavio Morlani. As on much of the Italian landscape, hills and stones challenged a farmer's strength every working day. But after six years Giovanni was able to buy twenty-seven acres from the count, including a drab two-story house with eighteen rooms. Later Pope John said, "I grew up in an atmosphere of self-sufficient poverty which makes few demands."

Church was the center of Roncalli family life. They not only went to mass each morning but twice on Sunday, and Father Francesco became a friend as well as a spiritual guide. It may have been the priest who suggested that Angelo should go to the school in Carvico, a little more than a mile away. School was an experience that not all poor Italian boys had, but Angelo's father recognized his son's natural intelligence.

Years later, recalling the one-room school in Carvico, Pope John said, "Grammar was pounded into my head with many a box on the ears." Whether or not he ever took to grammar was not as important as the fact that he took to reading. He read with excitement and joy, and in every waking hour. It was not long before his parents knew that they had a scholar, not a farmer, on their hands. Not only did he read, but he remembered the words with almost photographic accuracy.

5

In three years, Angelo had read through the shelved resources at Carvico. At the age of nine, he transferred to a secondary school at Celano, which meant a three-mile walk each day over the mountain and another three miles back home again each night. In winter, the trip was longer and harder. Between the physical strain and the more difficult subjects, Angelo's academic record left something to be desired. The family began to have doubts that the junior seminary at Bergamo would accept the boy when he reached the age of eleven.

At about this time, Giovanni and Maria Roncalli were dreaming the dream which many a devout Catholic parent has at one time or another for an outstanding son. They hoped that Angelo might become a priest. What they did not know was that young Angelo wanted the very same thing. In fact, years later he said, "I cannot remember a time when I did not want to serve God as a priest."

As his conviction became stronger, Angelo's prayers took on new vigor and his schoolwork grew more important to him. The dream of both parents and child was taking solid shape.

Perhaps it was because of the intensity of the dream that Count Morlani decided to pay the fees for Angelo to register at the seminary in Bergamo.

CHAPTER TWO

STAKE IN A DREAM

THE CITY OF BERGAMO, eight miles from Sotto il Monte, was a seat of religious scholarship and the pride of every Italian Catholic. Not all the students were preparing for the priesthood. Bergamo Seminary offered courses in the major professions, too. But Angelo's heart was set on becoming a priest. It was not hard for him to pass over mathematics and science in favor of Church history and philosophy. Bergamo introduced him not only to music and literature but to great examples of leadership in Monsignor Camillo Guindani, bishop of Bergamo, and laymen such as Nicolo Rezzara and Count Stanislao Medolago Albani.

Some of the boys complained about the Spartan schedule of early-to-bed, early-to-rise, endless prayers, chores, and poor food, but Angelo thrived. A poor farm-boy was used to hard work and meager meals.

The next three years passed happily for the boy, and on June 28, 1895, at the age of thirteen, Angelo's head was shaved as an act of intention toward the priesthood.

7

With his intention declared, Angelo exuded a simple inner joy which he never lost in the passing years. Along with his joy grew a warm genuine humility. But perhaps the most important result of his declared intention was the beginning of a personal spiritual diary —later to be called *Journal of a Soul*—which reveals the inner development of his life.

The first entry in the diary was made in 1895, after his head was shaved and he received the confidential "little rules" from his spiritual director, a cleric of Angelo's own choosing. The priest would provide guidance in Angelo's spiritual life.

As his adaptation of the "little rules," Angelo wrote and accepted some rules of his own when he was fourteen years old.

EVERY DAY

1. Devote at least a quarter of an hour to mental prayer as soon as you get out of bed in the morning.

2. Hear, or better, serve Holy Mass.

3. Devote a quarter of an hour to spiritual reading.

4. In the evening, before going to bed, make a general examination of conscience, followed by an act of contrition, and prepare the points for the next day's meditation.

5. Before dinner or before supper, or at least before the general evening examination, make a

particular examination concerning the best way to rid yourself of certain vices or failings and concerning the acquiring of certain virtues.

6. Be diligent in attending the meetings of the Sodality on feast days, in school and in study circles on week days, and always allow sufficient time for study when you are at home.

7. Visit the Blessed Sacrament and some church or chapel where there is a special devotion to the Blessed Virgin, at least once a day.

8. Recite five Our Fathers and five Hail Marys in honor of the wounds of Our Lord Jesus Christ, between 6 and 9 o'clock in the evening, and make at least three acts of self-mortification in honor of the Virgin Mary.

9. Recite the other vocal prayers and practice the other usual devotions to the Virgin Mary, to St. Joseph, to the patron saints and the Holy Souls. These devotions must however meet with the approval of your own director, as must also the books for meditation and spiritual reading.

10. Read carefully and thoughtfully a whole chapter, or at least a part of one, of the very devout Latin book of Thomas a Kempis [fifteenth-century German monk].

11. So as to be constant in your observation of these points, arrange the hours of your day, and set apart the special time for prayer, study and other devotions, for recreation and sleep, after consulting with your Spiritual Father.

12. Make a habit of frequently raising your mind to God, with brief but fervent invocations.

EVERY WEEK

1. Make your confession and communion.

2. Fast on Friday and Saturday.

3. On these days perform some penance, on the advice of your Spiritual Father.

4. On these days devote also an extra quarter of an hour to prayer or spiritual reading and this, if possible, in the quiet of some church. Instead of this you may give or attend some lectures on a spiritual subject, or perform any other act of piety substituted by your director at his choice.

5. When sitting or walking with one or more companions, discuss good and spiritual things. The subject for the discussion might be taken from the morning meditation, or from the spiritual reading, or from some of the Rules, sharing with others in friendly conversation the pious feelings these have aroused in you, or other feelings the Lord has inspired.

In addition, Angelo had specific rules for every month, every year, at special times, and at all times:

1. Above all other evils beware of bad or unworthy companions, those whose speech contains impure suggestions, filthy or cynical words, or dialect expressions. Avoid those who cultivate the

company of the other sex and talk about love-making; those who hang around in inns, or are intemperate, particularly in drinking; those who wish to be admired as revengeful, quarrelsome men, swift to draw a weapon; those who walk up and down or loiter in the squares and before the shops; those who go to gaming houses, or those who are known to be youths rebellious to good discipline, averse to study and given over to frivolous pastimes.

2. Never converse familiarly or play or jest or in any other manner show too much confidence with women, whatever may be their state in life, their age or relationship; never confide in them the slightest thing which might in any way be dangerous or suspect.

3. Never play at forbidden games or even at games which are permitted, such as those with cards or dice, and least of all in public where all sorts of people gather, and never linger to look on at these games.

4. On no account or pretext must you use the intimate "thou" in talking together or lay your hands on each other, or run after, push or strike each other, even in jest, nor should you indulge in other careless actions, words or gestures which might provoke scorn or be the cause of even greater danger.

During his years at Bergamo Seminary Angelo

visited his family on holidays. Their love for him never wavered even though they could not help him financially. But these vacations were often difficult because his parents were very indulgent of him. Once in a while his brothers and sisters became jealous when their parents curtailed the household noise so that Angelo might study or meditate. Once the situation became so serious that he recorded in his *Journal*:

> Only three days of the holidays have passed and already I am weary of them. At the sight of so much unhappiness in the midst of so much mistrust, oppressed by so many fears, often I sigh, sometimes I weep. What humiliations! I only try to do good, to love sincerely even those who seem to me not to wish me well, and perhaps they think of me as a wretched blackguard.

Later he wrote of the holidays:

> . . . as regards the trials of family life . . . renewed especially in these days of holiday, I have offered them all up to the Blessed Heart of Jesus, who is my love. He knows that I do not seek for my dear ones riches and pleasures but only patience and charity. He knows that, if I grieve, I grieve only for the lack, in them, of these virtues.

Angelo's acceptance of the "little rules," as well as his self-imposed laws, was accompanied by an unceasing spiritual search. The following are excerpts from *Journal* entries written when he was seventeen.

In March, 1898, he wrote: "In a word, I find that I am still at the beginning of the journey which I have undertaken, and this makes me feel ashamed. I thought I could have been a saint by this time, and instead I am still as miserable as before."

In April: "Holy Week has gone by, the vacation also is over, and instead of moving forward I have continued to slip back."

In May: "I will endeavor above all to keep my thoughts from wandering, so that I may watch over myself and little by little master my passions, especially my self-love."

In July: "Moreover, I waste too much time in the kitchen in idle chatter. I must also learn to control my curiosity about things which are nothing to do with me. I shall also take care not to doze during meditation, as I did this morning."

In August: "The other evening I had no candle, last night I had no ink, and so for two evenings running I have written nothing. When I look back over the last few days I must admit that even if I cannot find any serious faults to deplore, I cannot find any virtues either. I am still stuck in the same place, without moving a step forward."

In September: "Today I have done everything wrong. I have done no studying, but let that pass; I have omitted the particular examination of conscience, I have done little spiritual reading. In short, it is always like this with me.

13

"Also, in everything I do, I must behave like a boy, the boy I really am, and not try to pass myself off as a serious philosopher and a man of importance. It is my natural inclination to do that—this is what I am made of: pride!"

In late September Angelo learned of the death of Father Francesco, who had baptized him seventeen years before. "I am left an orphan, to my immense loss," he wrote. Then he prayed:

May the prayers which I know my good parish priest always said for me, for I believe I was his Benjamin [loyal son of Jacob in the Old Testament], and the prayers I now say for him, and his life which I shall always remember, make me truly like him. . . . I have succeeded in obtaining, as a precious token of remembrance of my priest, his *Imitation of Christ* [by Thomas a Kempis], the same volume he had used every evening since his seminarist days. To think he became holy, poring over this little book! . . . May I be strengthened by the example of my beloved and deeply mourned parish priest, for whom I implore eternal peace and glory.

Three years later, Angelo graduated with honors from the Bergamo Seminary, and Bishop Guindani presented him with a scholarship to the famous Seminario Romano. It was common knowledge that only the most promising young men received such an honor. It was also common knowledge that the seminary in Rome was a training ground for high Church officials. (One author referred to it as "the West Point of the Holy See.")

Angelo had done particularly well in Latin, theology, and philosophy during his years at Bergamo, but history was his favorite subject. Spiritually, his life was patterned after Saint Francis de Sales who had, two hundred years before, experienced the same joy and gentleness known to Angelo Roncalli.

CHAPTER THREE

A WIDENING WORLD

TWENTY-YEAR-OLD Angelo Roncalli first saw the city of Rome on January 3, 1901. This was a far different place from the small village of Sotto il Monte and the not-so-large city of Bergamo. Rome gave him a new dedication to his studies. His Bergamo teachers had believed in his ability, and he resolved not to let them down.

The seminary in Rome is often called Apollinaire, but, in 1937, its official title was changed to Political Lateran Institute of Higher Education. Its origins can be traced back to the Collegio Romano, founded by Saint Ignatius in 1551. Little wonder that Angelo was impressed with the historical aspects of such a place.

With growing excitement, he began his classes. His room was small, with one high, barred window. As in most cold, stone buildings, there was an ever-present dampness. But drab, musty buildings could not dampen his spirit. He found inspiring teachers and challenging courses, as well as new friends with whom he explored the historical city.

The new priest, shortly after he was ordained

Of all his courses, history continued to fascinate him. He studied canon law and the history of world religions, as well as the history of the Catholic Church.

Father Francesco Pitocchi, a gentle man, became Angelo's spiritual director. Later, Pope John referred to this relationship: "Ah, Padre Francesco! If later we managed to make something of our lives we must say it came from him."

Another teacher made an impression on him. This was Eugenio Pacelli, an assistant lecturer in canon law, and recognized by students for his great intellect. Pacelli was later to become Pope Pius XII.

17

Angelo's studies at the seminary were cut off in less than a year when he was taken into military service. Like other Italians of military age, he was given the opportunity to volunteer and select his branch of service. Angelo chose the infantry and volunteered with the 73rd Infantry Regiment, stationed at Bergamo.

Sergeant Roncalli found his living quarters better and more cheerful than the seminary in Rome. He also found the food more plentiful. But best of all, he was once again able to visit his family.

When his year of service ended, Angelo returned to Rome with greater determination than ever to do serious work.

On August 10, 1904, Angelo Roncalli was ordained a priest in the Church of Santa Maria in Monte Santo. The next day he celebrated his first mass at a small altar in St. Peter's Cathedral, which is next to the tomb of Saint Peter. Pope Pius X happened to see him that day. He touched the new priest on the head, and blessed him.

CHAPTER FOUR

WITH PEN IN HAND

WHEN RONCALLI had returned to Rome after his year of army life, he was even more eager to learn history. He was especially caught up in Church history—the people and events which moved the Church through the mainstream of the world.

Some of his reading prompted him to attempt writing books of his own. His works were not scholarly, nor widely read, and in later years, he said that they would have been lost forever had he not become pope.

His first book grew out of an essay on Caesar Baronius (1538–1607), a Church historian. Baronius was interested mainly in the early Church. A wise diplomat, he impressed Roncalli by his breadth of understanding and the spiritual atmosphere of his life.

At one time Baronius had met the church reformer Saint Philip Neri, who encouraged him to write a history of the early Church. It was this history that had impressed Roncalli.

At twenty-two, Baronius had become a cardinal, a high Church official ranking directly below the pope.

19

Baronius would walk daily to St. Peter's Basilica. Before entering, he gave a penny to each beggar outside, and then slipped inside to kiss the great bronze foot of Saint Peter. The statue has been kissed so often through the years that the toes are worn away. As Baronius kissed the foot he would say, *"Obedientia et pax"* (obedience and peace).

It is said that when Roncalli later became a cardinal, he went to St. Peter's, laid his forehead on the foot of the bronze statue, and repeated, *"Obedientia et pax."*

Roncalli's second literary attempt was a biography of his friend Radini-Tedeschi, bishop of Bergamo, whose warmth and intelligence had inspired the future pope. Years later, as Pope John, he spoke of the bishop as "my spiritual father" and "The Pole Star of my priesthood." Sometimes Roncalli was called "the shadow of the bishop." The two men were alike in that each was filled with a mixture of gentleness and vision.

Because of his relationship with Bishop Radini-Tedeschi, Roncalli was chosen by Pope Pius X to assist at the bishop's consecration, on January 29, 1905, the feast day of Saint Francis de Sales. During the ceremony, Roncalli laid the Book of the Gospels on the new bishop's shoulders. The book represented his acceptance of the yoke of Christ.

In one final, solemn moment, the pope embraced the newly consecrated bishop and whispered in his ear. No one knew what the pope had said for nine years. On his deathbed Bishop Radini-Tedeschi said to Father Roncalli, "Do you know what the pope whispered to me that day? He said, 'When you die I shall come for you and we will be together forever in Paradise.'" Then the bishop continued, "Our Holy Father is in Paradise now. I sense his voice. He is calling me and calling me. I will go to see him soon." He died two days after Pope Pius X.

As the bishop's secretary, Roncalli had accompanied him to the grotto in Lourdes, France, where Bernadette had seen the Blessed Virgin. The young priest loved Lourdes and made several return visits.

Besides Lourdes and other French shrines, Father Roncalli and Bishop Radini-Tedeschi visited Spain, Palestine, and all 352 parishes in the Bergamo diocese, where they learned not only the problems of the priests but the problems of the people.

On one trip they heard about striking factory workers who were in serious need of food as well as moral support for their cause. Most strikes revolve around poor salaries and working conditions, but this one concerned the right of labor to strike against the power of organized capital.

The bishop gave money and food to the strikers. He even called on them in their homes, which gave added moral support for their cause. To some people, such action was far beyond the realm of a bishop's job, and they became noisily irate.

Years later, Roncalli wrote: ". . . taking the side of the strikers was for him a highly Christian duty . . . and one of justice, charity, and social peace. So he let them scream and calmly continued [to support the strikers]."

The bishop's social concern never wavered and it rubbed off on Angelo Roncalli. For the rest of his life he was more than aware of human need in all its phases. Once he assisted the bishop in organizing thousands of laborers to travel abroad when unemployment in Italy was at an all-time high. They organized the League of Women Workers among women who had no legal rights in Italy at that time. They organized the Association for the Protection of Young Women, and an association for the protection of babies born out of wedlock.

In a diary entry on October 4, 1906, Roncalli recorded the message of a prayer given by the bishop as they had traveled the Holy Land. The prayer is significant because it clearly supports the deep and lasting influence of the bishop on the life of the young priest. Roncalli wrote:

All eyes were on the Bishop and all hearts responded to his words and throbbed in unison with his in one great prayer, the common desire shared by all that the separated brethren should return to the true fold.

With the help of all Christians everywhere why should today's prayer not become tomorrow's reality? Meanwhile we must strive for the realization of this wonderful prayer, so magnificently expressed, and leave the rest to God, knowing that Christ's words will one day come to pass, and especially here in Jerusalem: "one fold and one shepherd!"

Bishop Radini-Tedeschi spent his life interpreting the Gospel in a new, wide light to include the least of the brethren. Such an interpretation and its application was indeed a model for young Father Roncalli.

Not long after the bishop's death, Roncalli concentrated on writing about the life of his mentor. Since the death of Pope John XXIII, this publication has become available in an edition entitled, "Mons Giacomo Maria Radini Tedeschi." It contains letters and other papers related to life in Bergamo when Roncalli was the bishop's secretary.

His third book concerned Saint Charles Borromeo, cardinal-archbishop of Milan, who visited Bergamo in 1575.

In 1906, two years after Roncalli's ordination to the priesthood, he was appointed to lecture on Church history at the seminary in Bergamo. He became known as Don Angelo, and his students recalled him as an eager teacher bubbling with enthusiasm and humor. Some of them remembered his admonition: "Always be prepared to answer anyone who demands a reason for your faith."

One day, Don Angelo was asked by Bishop Radini-Tedeschi to go to Milan with him for a conference with the cardinal-archbishop. While his superiors talked, Roncalli browsed among the dusty books of

23

the archdiocese. There he discovered thirty-nine volumes relating the pastoral visits of Saint Charles Borromeo to Bergamo. He was overjoyed.

On the way back to Bergamo, Roncalli told the bishop of his excitement. The bishop recommended that he consult Monsignor Achille Ratti, prefect of the Ambrosiana Library in Milan, and later Pope Pius XI. This brilliant man almost overawed the young Don Angelo, and Ratti promised to look over the books. When he did, he recommended the sixth and seventh volumes to be of greatest interest for his eager student. Page after page was photostated and placed in chronological order for Roncalli's use.

For several years he worked on the Borromeo documents. Bishop Radini-Tedeschi became so excited over the project that he himself appropriated a small expense account for his young scholastic friend.

In 1909 Father Roncalli recorded in his spiritual diary:

Next year there will be great celebrations in Lombardy for the third centenary of the canonization of Saint Charles Borromeo; I have already tried to do something for him here in Bergamo, pointing out how richly the great Archbishop has earned our gratitude. I myself will try to make this great saint more and more familiar to my heart and mind, to pray to him frequently for his help and to imitate him. If, with the Lord's help, I could inspire the souls of our clergy with the example of

Saint Charles, it would do much to increase their eagerness for apostolic work, to the greater spiritual advantage of the whole diocese. Perhaps the work I have undertaken will be very onerous, but I will do it willingly in honour of Saint Charles, certain that in this way I shall be contributing more to the desired result.

CHAPTER FIVE

BOOKS VERSUS BATTLES

ITALY DECLARED WAR on Austria on May 24, 1915. For
Father Roncalli, it meant leaving Bergamo for Milan,
where he would be assigned to the medical corps.

He wrote in his diary:

Tomorrow I leave to take up my military service
in the Medical Corps. Where will they send me?
To the front perhaps? Shall I ever return to Bergamo, or has the Lord decreed that my last hour
shall be on the battlefield? I know nothing; all I
want is the will of God in all things and at all
times, and to work for his glory in total self-
sacrifice. In this way, and in this way only, can I
be true to my vocation and show in my actions
my real love for my country and the souls of my
fellows. My spirit is willing and cheerful. Lord
Jesus, keep me always so; Mary, my kind Mother,
help me "that in all things Christ may be
glorified."

At Milan, he was assigned to a medical unit based in Bergamo. The assignment seemed too good to be true.

But now Sergeant Roncalli saw the tragedies of war. He served both as nurse, friend, and priest to the young men returning from the front lines. It was an exhausting experience, physically as well as spiritually. He saw men afraid of life and afraid of death. He saw them cry over each other, hurt for each other, and pray for each other.

For awhile Sergeant Roncalli, with two gold sergeant-stripes on the sleeve of his cassock, tried to teach classes at the seminary along with his hospital work, but his pupils vanished into military service.

Many army officers did not like the soldier-priest arrangement, and one lieutenant colonel seemed to do everything he could to harass Sergeant Roncalli. Finally, near the end of the priest's military career, the man said, "Don't be offended by me, sergeant. You see, I am at bottom a poor man, glad to be able to add one more gold leaf to the visor of my kepi. You, on the other hand, are on your way to the top—monsignor, bishop, cardinal. . . ." They both laughed.

On March 28, 1916, all the soldier-priests in the Italian army were made chaplains and promoted to lieutenants. The war continued. The hospital in Bergamo overflowed with wounded men, and everyone worked nearly twenty-four hours a day. Finally, all the churches in Bergamo had to serve as wards to supplement the crowded hospital.

Pope John as a sergeant in the Italian medical corps, 1915

Lieutenant Roncalli served on the battlefield in 1917. He spoke of this as the most moving experience of his life. He moved with the troops "on the plateau of Asiago and the blood-soaked fields along the Piave."

Speaking of his chaplaincy years later, Pope John said, "The chaplain's is a deeply human and brotherly ministry where in the midst of fighting men the priest becomes the witness to the highest moral and religious ideals for which those valiant men have not hesitated to give their lives."

28

Near the end of his life he remarked: "I thank God that I was a sergeant and a military chaplain in World War I. How much I learned of the human heart at that time; how much experience I gained; how great the grace I received. . . ."

In November, 1918, World War I ended and Father Roncalli was discharged from military service. He received only a few hundred dollars after almost four years of work. Doctor Giuseppe Fumagalli paid him the money and apologized for the small amount. The young priest laughed and said, "Look, it's not much. But I can use it. I have a plan to open a students' clubhouse in Bergamo."

The Student House was one of the first, but not the last, in Italy. Roncalli obtained the old Palazzo Asperti and arranged the rooms so there was a chapel, recreation room, and sleeping quarters. It is said that he put a full-length mirror at the top of the stairs and hung above it the sign, "Know Thyself."

Father Roncalli loved being with the students, hearing their discussions, watching them struggle with their faith, and seeing them dedicate themselves anew to a good life.

By 1919, he was not only working at Student House and teaching at the seminary, but he was the spiritual adviser of the Union of Catholic Women, the Union of Catholic Youth, and the spiritual director of the Seminary itself.

At one point during this time Father Roncalli recorded in his diary:

During these last years there have been days when I wondered what God would require of me after the war. Now there is no more cause for uncertainty, or for looking for something else; my main task is here, and here is my burden, the apostolate among students. . . . So often, in the evening, when I turn over in my mind the events of the day spent in looking after my dear students, I feel in me something of the awe which fell upon those two disciples on the way to Emmaus, as if in contact with the divine.

CHAPTER SIX

OBEDIENTLY BACK
TO ROME

IN NOVEMBER, 1920, Angelo Roncalli, teacher, student-adviser, priest, and author, received a letter from Cardinal van Rossum in Rome, appointing him as director of the Society for the Propagation of the Faith in Italy. He was now thirty-nine years old. Thrilled as he was by the honor, he hated to leave Bergamo. But he knew that one did not dally very long over such an opportunity when the pope himself had directed the letter to be written.

The job concerned mission matters. It was hoped that Father Roncalli would bring about better coordination of the missions, for they had been greatly hampered during the war. It had been a difficult task for the missionary to preach love at a time when men's minds were concerned only with battle.

Angelo Roncalli worked at this job for four years. It was a discouraging task. One writer says:

Until 1917, the Congregation for the Propagation of the Faith had dealt with all Catholic priests

31

who worked in territories and countries where a majority of the population was non-Catholic, including those countries of Russia, Greece, Bulgaria, whose population belonged to the Eastern Orthodox churches. Pope Benedict XV decided that some visible expression should be given to the fact that the Eastern Orthodox churches were Catholicism's closest brothers—dissidents but brothers. There was no need to propagate the faith among them since they shared the faith. In founding the Congregation for the Oriental Church and the Oriental Institute, Benedict XV distinguished the matter of missionary work among non-Christians from that of work among members of the Oriental Church, whose bishops and priests were recognized as sharing the same priesthood as that of the Catholics.

Roncalli's work was made more difficult by the fact that there were three separate branches of missionary organizations and none of them had headquarters in Rome. Also the peoples of Africa and Asia were not so ready to trust the church after the war. New strategy was vital.

Shortly after Roncalli began his work, Pope Benedict XV died. The new pope was Achille Ratti, the librarian from Milan. He took the name of Pope Pius XI.

Some historians call Pope Pius XI one of the most important popes in all church history. It was certain that he was one of the most brilliant and most spiritual. In fact, to Roncalli, he seemed much like his own dear friend, Bishop Radini-Tedeschi. He knew the pope to be a man of deep faith and continuing concern for people in need.

In his diary, he recorded:

The Association for the Propagation of the Faith is the breath of my soul, and my life. Everything must be for this, and always: head, heart, spoken and written word, my prayers, labors and sacrifices, by day and night, in Rome and elsewhere, I repeat, everything and always. I will accept other priestly tasks only in so far as I can subordinate them and make them serve my primary mission, which is the only reason for my presence here in Rome.

Time and again Angelo Roncalli had proved to those about him that he was a natural-born organizer. He was efficient and quick, and he worked well with all kinds of people.

In 1921 the offices of the Propagation of the Faith were located on the Piazza di Spagna in an old Renaissance palace. It was not elegant, but it was adequate. One of Father Roncalli's first duties was to call upon the pope and see what he had in mind concerning the Propagation of the Faith. Roncalli was especially excited when he found that their meeting would take place in the papal apartment.

A biographer records their conversation: "The ways

of society are too old-fashioned to meet the dangerous conditions of modern times," the pope said. "We want you to reorganize it and bring it up to date. Impart to it some of your youthful vigor. But you must be tactful. You will meet opposition from the older men in the organization who have performed great services for the Church, but are now suffering the rigidity of age and are wedded to the old ways. You must make the innovations without hurting them. It will take much charity and patience. . . . We want you to visit all the important centers of the movement in Italy and in Europe to see what needs to be done. . . . You will be God's traveler."

The order must have seemed enormous, but travel he did. And along with his new work had come a new title. He was now Monsignor Roncalli.

Between 1922 and 1924, he made trips all over Europe. He tried to create new concern in missionary work, procure money, medical supplies, books and other equipment for missionary use, and help establish and fortify trust among the people. He hoped, too, that headquarters of the several branches might be moved to Rome.

Munich, Amsterdam, Brussels, Paris, Vienna, and other cities in Europe were on his itinerary. Roncalli made not one but many trips to these places, speaking, conferring, and coordinating efforts and enthusiasm about missionary work. He also published a magazine called *The Propagation of Faith in the World*. Some of the articles and speech reprints were again published in 1959, because they were just as relevant then as when Monsignor Roncalli had first written them.

Wherever he went, people seemed to like him, and he returned their affection. His jovial winsomeness made him a natural ambassador for the Church. Finally, some of the organization's branches did move their headquarters to Rome, and China was opened to missionary endeavors. This was partly the result of the fact that Confucianism was now proclaimed a philosophy instead of a religion, and almost overnight Protestants and Catholics poured missionary efforts into China. Schools, medical centers, and churches were erected, and a whole new atmosphere emerged concerning the missions.

After three years as director of the Society for the Propagation of the Faith, Monsignor Roncalli wrote in his diary:

Today is the third anniversary of my coming to Rome to take up my work on behalf of the Association for the Propagation of the Faith. My thoughts turn reverently to the Chair of Saint Peter, whence every apostolate draws its motive and life. In this beautiful place of meditation and rest, whence I can see the majestic dome, I hail that Chair of truth and pay it the fervent homage of my mind and heart.

A day of wonderful sunshine! The sparrows are chirping in the warm air. It is a delight to hear them, and the song of the bells in Saint Peter's.

Roncalli's work with the Society for the Propagation of the Faith brought him more and more in contact with Pope Pius XI. He visited the pope after trips, and reported on activities, problems, and plans. The pope respected Roncalli's work, and recognized his tremendous gift to work with people. He respected the priest's ability to organize, and his healthy stature which allowed him to be active and happy.

Out of recognition of these attributes, the pope appointed Monsignor Roncalli as a member of the Central Committee of the Holy Year (1925). The committee organized every detail of Holy Year activities—transportation, building construction, public relations, pilgrimages, and conference sessions. Roncalli was to direct the missionary exhibition, which would present the life and work in missions throughout China, Australia, Latin America, and Africa.

When the exhibit was finally opened, it showed the tremendous effort by hundreds of dedicated priests. Life-size wax figures dressed in native costumes brought each geographical area to life. Native arts were displayed. Missions were traced by charts. Brochures were printed and distributed, showing maps of missionary endeavor.

The exhibit was a tremendous success, and the pope was pleased. He praised all those who had worked so hard to present such an accurate pictorial presentation to the public.

During this period, Roncalli was also teaching

classes at the seminary in Rome. He taught patristics, which covers the early history of the Church, especially the first twelve centuries.

Busy as he was, Monsignor Roncalli was always first and foremost a priest in his own mind, and his personal spiritual quest never ceased.

At this point, he wrote in his spiritual diary:

What have I done for Christ? Little, little or nothing. What am I doing for Christ? Something, but badly, like a sluggard. What should I do for Christ? Everything, O Lord, if you do but help me with your holy grace. . . . Say it quite clear: to love God, not myself; to do the will of God, not my own, and work for the good of others, not for my own, and all this always, everywhere and with great joy. . . .

CHAPTER SEVEN

THE MAN AND HIS SOUL

AN INTEGRAL PART of the life of Pope John XXIII was his search to know God, to love more deeply, to serve more adequately. He cannot be understood without understanding his religious feelings. They begin with his spiritual diary, *Journal of a Soul*, started when he was fourteen years old. It contains not only his spiritual search but his last will and testament, special prayers for special events, people, and places, and devout thoughts on the rosary.

At seventeen he recorded, "I really need a good box on the ears. These last two evenings it could almost be said that I have not made my visit, at least not one of a decent length. I am not to blame for this, because obedience obliged me to go elsewhere, but if I had followed the impulse, which I occasionally feel, to make this visit a little earlier in the day, then there would have been nothing to be sorry about."

In November of that year he wrote, "I am good at thinking up virtues, not at practicing them. . . ." And later that same month, "Beware of talking about other

38

people and above all sitting in judgment on Tom, Dick, and Harry."

When he was nineteen he wrote:

Who am I? Where do I come from? Where am I going? I am nothing. Everything I possess, my being, life, understanding, will and memory—all were given me by God, so all belong to Him. Twenty short years ago all that I see around me was already here; the same sun, moon and stars, the same mountains, seas, deserts, beasts, plants and men; everything was proceeding in its appointed way under the watchful eyes of Divine Providence. And I? I was not here. Everything was being done without me, nobody was thinking of me, nobody could imagine me, even in dreams, because I did not exist.

And you, O God, with a wonderful gesture of love, you who are from the beginning and before all time, you drew me forth from my nothingness, you gave me being, life, a soul, in fact all the faculties of my body and spirit; you opened my eyes to this light which sheds its radiance around me, you created me. So you are my Master and I am your creature. I am nothing without you, and through you I am all that I am. I can do nothing without you; indeed if at every moment you did not support me I should slip back whence I came, into nothingness. This is what I am. . . . God created me. Yet he did not need me; the whole

scheme of the universe, the world which sur-
rounds me, everything, in fact, would exist without any help from me.

Why then do I think myself so necessary to this
world? What am I but an ant or a grain of sand?
Why do I puff myself up so proudly? Arrogance,
pride, self-esteem! What am I set in this world to
do? To serve God. He is my supreme Master
because he has created me, because he preserves
my life, and so I am his servant. Therefore my
whole life must be consecrated to him, to carry
out his wishes, in all things and at all times. So,
when I do not think of God, when I attend to my
own comforts, my own self-love, my good esteem
among men, I neglect my most compelling duty, I
become a disobedient servant. And what will God
do with me then? O Lord, do not strike me with
the thunderbolts of your justice, and do not dismiss me from your service, as I would only too
well deserve. . . .

This dedicated thinking set the tone for the entire
life of Angelo Roncalli. He was God's servant, His
child, His creation. He felt called by God. He did not
hear voices as did Joan of Arc, nor receive the stigmata
(the wounds of Christ on the cross) as did Saint
Francis of Assisi. But he knew just as clearly that God
had called and intended to use him for a purpose.

At twenty-one, Angelo Roncalli wrote about his
servanthood:

Who am I? Nothing. What is my name? What are my titles of nobility? I have none. I am a servant and nothing more. I have nothing of my own, not even my life. God is my Master, absolute Master over life and death. No parents, no relations, no masters in this world. My real and only Master is God.

So, I live only to obey God's slightest commands. I cannot move a hand, a finger or an eye, I cannot look before me or behind, unless God wills it. In his presence I stand upright and motionless, like the meanest soldier standing to attention before his officer, ready to do all, even to cast myself into the flames. This must be my task my whole life long, because I was born for this: I am a servant.

In that same year, mindful of his youth, he wrote, "There is still too much of the dust of battle about me. Youthful enthusiasms, radiant ideals, splendid visions; these dreams are very beautiful but must for the present be handled with care. They could lead to a waste of time, however excellent and holy they may be in themselves. . . ."

At twenty-two he recorded, "Today was a perfect feast; I spent it in the company of St. Francis de Sales, my gentlest of saints. What a magnificent figure of a man, priest and Bishop! If I were like him, I would not mind even if they were to make me Pope!"

During a retreat that same year he wrote, ". . . The Church has called me, you invite me: 'Lo I come.' I have no pretensions, I have no preconceived plans, I am trying to strip myself of all that is self, I am no longer my own. My soul is open before you, like a blank sheet of paper. Write on it what you will, O Lord: I am yours."

At thirty-eight, as director for the Propagation of the Faith, he wrote:

I pledge myself especially to seek perfect poverty of spirit in absolute detachment from myself, never feeling any anxiety about positions, career, distinctions or anything else. Am I not already too much honored in the sublime simplicity of my priesthood and in the work I am doing now, not sought by me but entrusted to me by Providence, by the voice of my Superiors?

I dwell at length on this matter because it is fundamental for my welfare. I will never say or do anything, I will dismiss as a temptation any thought, which might in any way be directed to persuading my Superior to give me positions or duties of greater distinction. . . .

Such entries continue throughout the entire diary. He was ever mindful of his calling and of his personal joy in being called to serve not as a master but as a servant. He sought humility, simplicity, evenness of spirit, perfection of intentions, and disciplined devotion.

At seventy he recognized himself on the threshold of eternity and was as aware of the mystery of life as at the age of twenty-one. "I want to be a holy pastor," he wrote, and so he became to the whole world.

CHAPTER EIGHT

PRIESTLY DIPLOMACY

In 1925 Italy was a country of changing politics, religion, and social awareness. It was a Holy Year with its air of religious festivities, but also a political year of disintegration. Twenty-five years before there had been much fervor over whether or not Catholics could belong to political parties and vote. But by 1925 the party system had broken down and the issue had settled itself. Benito Mussolini, a Fascist, was the prime minister, and he erased all political parties except his own and put an end to parliamentary democracy.

During this period of change, Pope Pius XI kept close watch on the world Church, recognizing that each nation had its own unique problem.

One of the most urgent problems before him was that of Bulgaria. Catholics were greatly outnumbered by Eastern Orthodoxy, and the Vatican administrator of the Latin-rite Catholics in Sofia had died. Without an administrator, the pope had no voice in the Bulgarian capital. On March 3, 1925, Pope Pius decided to appoint Angelo Roncalli as apostolic visitor to Bulgaria. In order to legalize the appointment according to Church rules, Monsignor Roncalli had to be given the rank of archbishop.

The title of archbishop is an honorary rank, bestowed by the pope, and it must be attached to a geographical site. After much consideration Pope Pius XI decided to make Roncalli the titular archbishop of Areopolis, an extinct diocese in Palestine (it had been taken over by the Arabs).

Roncalli took his new assignment with *"Obedientia et pax,"* saying, "In reality, to be named a bishop or to remain a simple priest is no different to those who seek only the glory of the Lord and not the evanescent glitter of earthly satisfaction."

Within a few days he was relieved of his duties with the Society for the Propagation of the Faith and all other activities.

Consecration as a bishop is one of the most solemn ceremonies of the Roman Catholic Church, and he went to the Villa Carpegna in Rome for several days of spiritual preparation.

On March 17, two days before his consecration day, he recorded these words in his diary:

I have not sought or desired this new ministry: the Lord has chosen me, making it so clear that it is his will that it would be a grave sin for me to refuse. So it will be for him to cover up my failings and supply my insufficiencies. This comforts

45

me and gives me tranquillity and confidence.
. . . The world has no longer any fascination for
me. I want to be all and wholly for God, pene-
trated with his light, shining with love for God
and the souls of men. . . . The Church is making
me a Bishop in order to send me to Bulgaria, to
fulfil there, as Apostolic Visitor, a mission of
peace. Perhaps I shall find many difficulties awaiting me. With the Lord's help, I feel ready for
everything. I do not seek, I do not desire, the
glory of this world; I look forward to greater glory
in heaven.

The episcopal motto he accepted was *Obedientia et
pax*.

On March 19, 1925, in the church of San Carlo al
Corso (named after Saint Charles Borromeo) and before parents, friends, and a delegation from the Bergamo Seminary, Angelo Roncalli was consecrated a
bishop.

One biographer says:

As he went through the long, beautifully symbolic ceremony Roncalli was swept by torrents of
strong emotion—awe, fear of unworthiness, high
resolve, and total submission to the will of God.
At last it was ended. He stood there wearing the
miter, which is the old Mosaic symbol of leadership, and holding the crozier signifying the Shepherd. On his finger was the episcopal ring to

symbolize his marriage to his flock; around his neck hung the jeweled pectoral cross, emblem of his faith in Christ and his readiness to die for this faith. He stood there and trembled. . . .

Following the same pattern as when he was ordained, Bishop Angelo Roncalli went to St. Peter's Basilica and celebrated his first mass at the altar over the tomb of Saint Peter. Later that day he was blessed by the pope, and then went to Sotto il Monte for rest. While he was there he arranged for two of his sisters to follow him to Bulgaria and keep house for him.

On April 25, Archbishop Roncalli arrived in Sofia, Bulgaria, with his secretary Father Constantino Bosschaerts.

Sofia was being harassed by terrorists, and one of Roncalli's first duties was to call on more than three hundred persons wounded in an explosion.

The new archbishop was well aware that Roman Catholics in Bulgaria were greatly outnumbered by Greek and Russian Orthodox believers. The Russian Church did not submit to the authority of the pope and had a code of canon law that was both different and unacceptable to the Roman Church. Besides these groups, 300,000 refugees from Macedonia had entered the city after a Turkish invasion. It is estimated that some 20,000 of them were Catholics with their own bishop. It was the job of Archbishop Roncalli to reconcile all these segments and help them to come together

47

as a blessing to each other. The order was a big one, which seemed to call more for a miracle than diplomacy.

His first sermon gave the key to his approach. "It is not enough to have the kindest feelings toward our separated Christian brothers," he told his Catholic flock. "If you really love them, give them a good example, and translate your love into action."

Within four days Bulgaria's King Boris accepted Archbishop Roncalli as an official caller. The two men liked each other right away and became friends, although it was Boris who would later give the archbishop his greatest headache in Bulgaria.

For the next ten years Roncalli represented the pope among Bulgarian Catholics. He visited them in hospitals, prisons, and tiny villages. He visited farmers, bankers, churchmen. He toured military posts and mosques. He forded rivers, slept on cots, rode workhorses, waded through mud, rowed boats, and walked across rugged mountains. Once he was advised to leave his ring and cross behind because the highways were crawling with bandits. (He obeyed.) Some had called him "God's traveler," and he was just that.

Roncalli visited every Catholic church and chapel, reminding the faithful that they had not been forgotten in Rome. Everywhere he went people were drawn to this warm, congenial man. The smile on his face and twinkle in his eye deepened their belief in his sincerity. Archbishop Roncalli was the first ranking representative of the pope to visit Bulgaria in six hundred years.

While he dealt with intricate maneuverings over such problems as the language for prayers, or French missionary claims in the Balkans, he kept insisting that he was a priest and not a diplomat. Perhaps this was a part of the key to his acceptance by the people. Archbishop Roncalli also learned the Bulgarian language, and he knew the country's history.

Seven years after his arrival in Bulgaria, Pope Pius raised Roncalli to the rank of apostolic delegate. It was still a nondiplomatic title, but it enhanced the position of Rome in the eyes of the Bulgarians. The king himself was happy about the recognition to his country.

But a break in good relations between King Boris and the apostolic delegate came when the king married the daughter of Victor Emmanuel III, of Italy. Boris belonged to the Orthodox Church and Giovanna to the Roman Catholic. There was no doubt that in mixed marriages such as this, the wedding had to be performed in a Catholic church, and that all children of the union were to be raised as Catholic. The non-Catholic partner was required to sign a written statement to this effect, and that he (or she) would not interfere with the children's Catholic education.

Boris agreed to all this even though he was Orthodox and so were eighty-five percent of his countrymen. The couple was married in Assisi, Italy, in the rite of the Catholic Church. Archbishop Roncalli helped to bring off the smooth plans for the wedding and its many political-religious intricacies.

Everything went as arranged until the newlyweds arrived home, where the king and Giovanna were remarried in an Orthodox ceremony. When their first son was born he was baptized an Orthodox.

Some Bulgarians saw this as the king's only way of keeping peace among his people. Others saw it as a way to merge Orthodoxy with Roman Catholicism. Still others felt that the king had broken a promise. Naturally, Roncalli was dismayed at the king's actions.

Despite the headaches suffered over the king's marriage, Archbishop Roncalli did accomplish several important tasks during his years in Bulgaria. The government began to recognize diplomas awarded by Catholic schools; two dioceses of Latin rites were brought together; Roncalli received permission to start a Catholic seminary in Bulgaria, and planted seeds for new Catholic schools, churches, and other religious institutions. Six churches were completely rebuilt, five new churches were built, and many were restored.

In 1934, nearly ten years after his appointment to Bulgaria, Archbishop Roncalli learned that he would be promoted to the rank of nuncio (top diplomatic envoy of the pope), and would be named apostolic delegate to Turkey and Greece. He was stunned. And so were his Bulgarian friends.

Newspapers eulogized him and friends wept over his departure. One old Byzantine priest said, "Monsignor, you have shown to us the gentleness of David and the wisdom of Solomon."

On Christmas Day, 1934, Roncalli, speaking in Bulgarian, gave the following as a part of his farewell address, broadcast from the Church of the Capuchin Fathers in Sofia:

. . . Leaving for the new post to which I have been assigned I carry with me a precious remembrance of Bulgaria. I have asked the Holy Father to change my titular archbishopric to that of a marvelous place, which is truly a jewel of Bulgaria. From now on I shall no longer bear the title of Archbishop of Areopolis but shall be known as the Archbishop of Mesembria. Thus each day I shall be reminded of Bulgaria, a remembrance that will echo in my heart each time I raise my hand solemnly to bless the people and every time I sign a document.

And you, my beloved brother, do not forget me . . . who will always remain, beyond wind and sea, the fervent friend of Bulgaria. There is a tradition in Catholic Ireland that on Christmas Day each family puts a lighted candle in the window of their home, so that if Saint Joseph and the Virgin Mary should be passing by they may know that within, beside a fire and a table blessed by the Grace of God, the family awaits them.

Wherever I may be throughout the world, if a

Bulgarian, who might be in distress, should pass my house, he will find the candle of welcome burning in the window. Let him knock on my door and it will be opened to him, whether he is Catholic or Orthodox. My Bulgarian brother, you have only to enter to find my house the warmest and most affectionate hospitality. . . .

At one point in his talk he said, "As for me, I have done very little for you. I failed in many respects, because of my defects, because of the limited possibilities and often because of my negligence, and though I tried to avoid offending anybody, please forgive me for all this as good brothers forgive. I am a man like you."

He left them with a smile amid his tears, but those who heard him that day knew that he was no ordinary man, no ordinary priest. He had the perspective on what it meant to be a servant of God.

CHAPTER NINE

MUCH WORK WAITING

"I AM IN TURKEY. . . . There is so much work waiting for me here! I bless God who fills me with the joys of his sacred ministry."

Filled with happy memories of Bulgaria, Archbishop Roncalli arrived in Istanbul on January 4, 1935. He was forty-seven years old. His welcome was not unlike his arrival in Sophia—quiet, unannounced, and attracting little attention.

One priest met him at the station and took him by taxi to the apostolic residence. The house was big and barnlike with not much homey atmosphere. His sisters would continue to keep house for him.

In Bulgaria, it was hard to remember that Roncalli had not held legal diplomatic status, for his relationship with King Boris had granted him so many diplomatic courtesies. In Turkey, this was quite reversed. He was representing the pope in Rome, and many Turks did not like Rome, the pope, or Catholics in general. In fact, the Turkish government was against anything religious, whether Catholic, Mohammedan, or Orthodox. Their antireligious stand was enforced so strictly that priests of any faith were required to wear business suits. The rule excluded the heads of churches, but Roncalli decided to conform and wear a business suit with a clerical collar.

Jealousies ran high for the loyalty of citizens. Kemal Atatürk's government was afraid of powerful religious leaders. From the very beginning, Turkey was difficult for Roncalli, and Greece was not much easier.

Due to his limited diplomatic activities, Archbishop Roncalli spent most of his time being a pastor to his Turkish flock. He counted about ten thousand in the fold, who followed the Latin rites and revered Pope Pius XI in Rome. There were other Catholics there who followed the rites but ignored the pope. Besides these people, Roncalli had sixty-seven priests and forty-nine churches under his wing. Such responsibilities would be enough for any man, but these duties would have been light if it had not been for the government's intervention.

Within two days after his arrival Angelo Roncalli gave a sermon to convince the people that he loved them and to show the government that he did not intend to interfere with policy. He said:

During these last few weeks I have had to fight a battle in my heart while leaving other brothers and sons who for ten years have been the object of my care and who were always a source of consolation to me—I wish to emphasize this and

54

repeat it to their credit—and whom I shall never
cease to love as long as I shall live. But now my
heart opens like arms to bless and leans toward
you who are to form my new spiritual family.
. . . You know very well, and all the world
knows well, that I have not been sent here to deal
in politics or look after material interests; my
functions are absolutely and exclusively religious.
And it is on these grounds that I wish to and must
remain at all cost.

He intended to stay. That was clear from the beginning. He accepted the Turkish strict policy of separa-
tion between church and state, as he moved among his
people.

Catholic schools were a major concern to him. He
did everything he could to expand their programs and
improve the quality of teaching.

Angelo Roncalli did not meet Kemal Atatürk, but
they each knew of the other. Special recognition came
secondhand from Atatürk when Roncalli ordered certain prayers and sermons to be given in the Turkish
language. This did not meet with full approval in
Rome.

The Turkish undersecretary of the foreign office
once said to him: "The secularity of the state is our
fundamental principle and the guarantee of our
liberty."

Roncalli replied: "The Church will be careful not to
infringe your liberty . . . but I am most optimistic.

In every case I aim for that which unites rather than that which separates. So we are in accord."

As difficult as his job was, Roncalli wrote in his diary: "I want to study Turkish with more care and perseverance. I am fond of the Turks, to whom the Lord has sent me; and it is my duty to do what I can for them. . . ."

He never lost his sense of direction. *Obedientia et pax* carried him along in all his work.

During his first year in Turkey, Roncalli's father died on August 2, 1935, at the age of eighty-one. The archbishop returned home briefly to be with his family.

After he came back, he also had problems with Greece as well as Turkey. There, too, the government scarcely noticed his presence. The Greek Orthodox Church was as anti-Rome as the Orthodox Church in Turkey. To do his work, Roncalli almost tiptoed among his flock of fifty thousand Catholics.

Above all else he was aware of their poverty. Jobs, food, clothing, and housing were scarce. The archbishop gasped over the conditions, and tried to help his spiritual children.

"My mission in Greece, oh what a burden! Yet for that very reason I love it the more and intend to carry it on with fervor, forcing myself to overcome all my repugnance. . . ."

He helped to feed the hungry, clothe the naked, visit the sick, pray with the dying, and preach love to all. Everywhere he went people responded to his warm sympathy and tenderness. He organized groups for practical economic action, and alleviated some of the human suffering. All the while he was striving for the relaxation of legal strings against new schools and churches. But the government, beset by unrest, did not wish to deal with relaxing anything when the times called for tightening up.

A 1936 attempt to overthrow the government led by General John Metaxas brought even greater tightening of the laws. Now it was almost impossible to carry on any religious work whatsoever.

In time, Angelo Roncalli made friends with Greece's King George II, just as he had with King Boris. The laws were modified. It was a great diplomatic victory.

This was followed by events that, years later, turned out to be vital.

The Greek Orthodox Church and the Church of England announced their acceptance of each other. They agreed to recognize the validity of each other's Holy Orders. It looked like quite a strong coalition had formed against the Greek Catholic Church, and people were interested in the reaction of Archbishop Roncalli. To their surprise he said, "I have nothing but praise for our separated brothers for their zeal in taking a step toward the union of all Christians." His statement was electrifying. Was it true that he, too, recognized the Church of England as being really Christian?

As Pope John, he would answer the question in the affirmative.

The year of 1939 was a difficult one for Angelo
Roncalli. In February came the death of his dear
friend Pope Pius XI. In August, his mother died. In
September, Hitler marched on Poland, and suddenly
the world was at war again.

At the requiem mass for Pope Pius XI in Istanbul,
the archbishop spoke of the secret longing held by the
late pope—the unity of all Christians. He preached:
"Time veils and unveils everything. . . . The day will
come, perhaps it is still very far, when the vision of
Christ of one shepherd and one flock will become the
lovely reality of earth and heaven."

In March, 1939, the new pope was named. Roncalli
was surprised and pleased to learn that the next head
of the church was to be Eugenio Pacelli, the brilliant
lecturer at Bergamo Seminary. Roncalli remembered
the new pope as a brilliant scholar moving in a world
of diplomacy and vast knowledge. For nine years before his election to the papacy, Pacelli had been the
papal secretary of state. The Catholic world put much
trust in this man, whose ability, they felt, could guide
them through the storm which raged across the world.
Pacelli chose the name Pope Pius XII.

A new pope could make new choices for papal
representatives. But Roncalli stayed on, and no word
came of a successor. The only word that did come,
along with the news of his mother's death in Sotto il
Monte, was the news of war.

Europe fell into chaos. Turkey was neutral but it
became a direct link between Europe and Asia Minor.

Roncalli was caught up in the dedicated business of trying to save human life. As one biographer stated: "Roncalli's delegation became one of the most important clearing houses for tens of thousands of queries from anxious men and women of all the warring nations and of all religions—and none—about their loved ones who had disappeared in the war."

In Istanbul, he was aware of spies spying on spies. "I learned to recognize them all," he remarked.

Roncalli never got over the Nazi purge of the Jews, and through his efforts with the Vatican he saved the lives of thousands of Jewish children who had escaped from Germany into Constantinople, which tried to maintain its neutrality by ordering them shipped back. But seeing their danger and certain death, Roncalli helped the government to decide to send them to another neutral country rather than back into Germany.

Later, Franz von Papen, German ambassador in Turkey, helped Roncalli to save the lives of Jews by getting them into Palestine. It is said that Roncalli tried to help von Papen when the German was tried at Nuremburg after the war, and fifteen years later Pope John granted him a private Vatican audience.

Politically, the war did not scar Turkey, but Greece was in enemy hands from 1941 on, causing even greater hardship among the Greeks. The land was stripped of its crops and no one had enough to eat. Thousands of youth were in stockades, and the nation was chained by its captors, Germany and Italy. The situation looked hopeless, and Roncalli felt that it was. There was nothing he could do.

Finally, he met with the head of the Greek Orthodox Church. "A thousand Greeks are dying every day of starvation. We must do something," said the Orthodox representative.

"We will," said Roncalli.

A plan was worked out for the Allied nations to ship in 370,000 tons of wheat to alleviate the suffering.

Another time, the Orthodox leader sent a letter to Pope Pius XII imploring his aid for the starving Greek nation. The requested help came.

At the last meeting between Roncalli and the Orthodox leader, they parted with the kiss of peace, the symbol in the Catholic and Orthodox liturgy of forgiving love. Such a gesture broke a thousand years of separateness. For Roncalli, this historic moment may have been great enough to foreshadow an ever-strengthening philosophy concerning the separated brethren.

Greece needed more than physical aid. She needed a morale builder and leadership. She needed to rid herself of enemies within and without. Turkey, too, had suffered, although her cities were not bombed. In December, 1944, the world seemed weak and confused. Peace was a vague hope even though the Allied armies had moved over France, and Italy had moved farther away from Nazi domination.

Such times must be especially black for those who believe in love, kindness, and peace for all people. It must have been a time of wondering for Archbishop Roncalli—a time of recalling his mistakes and rethinking his strategy. It may also have been a time for thinking of his future.

The following is a general outline of a last will and testament made during these days in Istanbul:

To the Holy Father for the Vatican Library my whole collection of things of Bergamesque interest, not only as an act of homage but so that my example may serve as an encouragement to others, in other dioceses in Italy and abroad, to do the same for the increase and adornment of that famous library.

To the Bishop of Bergamo, to adorn his residence where I spent the first happy years of my priesthood as secretary to Msgr. Radini-Tedeschi of revered memory, to whom I owe so much, the large canvas, 'Our Lady with the Child and the little St. John'. . . .

To the Cathedral of Bergamo, where I always enjoyed the cherished privilege of remaining a Canon, although an unworthy one, even after I was made a Bishop, I bequeath my ceremonial cope of silk with the ermine. This ermine belonged to the late Msgr. Radini-Tedeschi. . . . The cope may be used on the funeral catafalque of Bishops or Canons.

To the seminary of Bergamo, so dear to me, where I remained for 25 years a student and teacher, my silver crozier, the small panel portrait of Msgr. Radini-Tedeschi . . . and all my manuscripts. . . .

To the parish church of Sotto il Monte, which I should so much have liked to help more generously, my gold watch and chain, and two crosses . . . so that they may be sold and the proceeds used to provide a large well-designed, artistic, silver chalice. . . .

All the books that I myself have acquired and possess at the time of my death shall stay in Istanbul. They will be of use to my successors. . . .

As for my body, I beg the Holy Father to have the kindness to arrange for it to be transported to my native place, Sotto il Monte, and buried there in the parish church. . . .

One day in December, 1944, a coded telegram reached Roncalli's office in Istanbul. On that day, Roncalli's secretary happened to be away. Thinking the message to be routine diplomatic business, the archbishop decoded it. Halfway through, he realized that he was being sent as papal nuncio to Paris. Aloud he said, "I think that they have lost their minds in Rome." But he knew enough about Vatican appointments to know that the pope himself was responsible.

In late December, Roncalli left his post in Istanbul after nearly twenty years in the Balkans. Some of those years had been the hardest of his ministry. But he had maintained an ever-widening perspective on the mission of the Church, its separated brethren, and the difficulties of the Church amid secularism. These facts would become vitally important to him in fifteen years.

CHAPTER TEN

THE DELICATE BALANCE

AFTER ENCOUNTERING the antireligious feeling in Turkey and the starving in Greece, one might have thought that Angelo Roncalli deserved an easier job than France. Actually, he was chosen as papal nuncio to France because of his wealth of diplomatic experience in difficult situations. France was in such a position, and the pope needed an experienced man.

Who knows better than experienced diplomats the delicate balance that must be kept in international relationships? Roncalli had been a diplomat in Turkey, where religions were scarcely tolerated, as well as a personal representative of the pope. He had performed magnificently. Who was better qualified to go to France?

It was the French custom on New Year's Day for the entire diplomatic corps to call on the president en masse. One ambassador made a speech for the entire group. The spokesman was either the papal nuncio (if there was one) or the ambassador who had been in France the longest.

64

In December, 1944, the Vatican was in the process of changing nuncios, and the oldest ambassador happened to be from the Soviet Union. It suddenly dawned upon the other diplomats that the Soviet ambassador was to be their spokesman and they did not want him to be. It was a crucial moment in diplomacy.

The urgency became so great that, on December 29, the French government sent a military plane to Istanbul, picked up Nuncio Roncalli, and flew him to Paris on December 30.

The next day, he presented his credentials to President Charles de Gaulle, and on January 1, 1945, appeared in the full regalia of the episcopacy to read the speech of the diplomatic corps.

Later he wrote a friend: "I seemed to be seized by surprise, like Habakkuk, and transported suddenly from Istanbul to Paris by a sort of incantation. Also my interior discipline was turned topsy-turvy . . . the more so since it seemed absolutely incredible to me and certainly I had neither the courage nor the imagination nor the desire for it. I was stupefied. . . ."

Perhaps his entrance into France set the pace for what would follow during the next eight years.

While looking forward to making new friends, Roncalli was thrown into the midst of a decision over thirty-three bishops who were accused of collaborating with the Nazi-controlled government in France during the German occupation. Valerio Valeri, the papal nuncio at the time, was ordered to Vichy, where

65

the government was, which literally meant supporting the Germans. The archbishop of Paris, and archbishops and bishops all over France remained at their posts, as the Church ordered them to do, and carried on their work under foreign-occupation rules. This meant that they received Catholic Germans into their congregations. In doing so they were following the rules of the Church as specified during all war situations.

The trouble came when France was liberated and leaders of the Resistance became the government leaders under General de Gaulle. A Catholic himself, de Gaulle felt obliged to ask the pope to recall Valeri and to remove thirty-three bishops from their posts. Valeri was released, but the issue of the bishops had to be discussed diplomatically.

Roncalli asked the government to make formal charges so that he might know and examine the full case. A great amount of material came to him, and after much consideration Roncalli said to de Gaulle: "What I have here is mostly newspaper clippings and gossip. These are not evidence in any system of justice. If you can't supply something more concrete, I am afraid that any action against these men would be discreditable both to me and to the justice of France." De Gaulle agreed, and only three bishops were removed.

When this matter was settled, Roncalli became more and more aware of his need for a place to invite friends and entertain. Paris seemed to require more of this than had Istanbul.

After careful house-hunting, he bought a lovely house in Paris at 10 Avenue Woodrow Wilson. The former owner was the prince of Monaco. The house needed paint and plaster, but refurbishing became a happy break in his diplomatic routine. Happily, he walked from room to room watching, advising, and impatiently waiting for it to be finished.

The living room could hold a large reception, but it was also cozy enough for intimate chats with friends. The dining room could seat fifty people on special occasions.

Roncalli entertained some of the most famous names in postwar France—Georges Bidault, the French foreign minister; Paul Henri Spaak; Winston Churchill; General Eisenhower; and many French cabinet members. It is said that they loved his wonderful sense of humor and that he was a gracious host. Like most gourmets, Roncalli knew the best in French delicacies, including wines and cigars. From time to time, he even hired Roger, said to have been the best chef in Paris.

Hundreds of social invitations were sent to Roncalli, and he accepted as many as possible. Making friends was part of the job of all diplomats. In fact, his work with the French laity raised not only the status of the laity, but also the status of the entire Catholic Church in postwar France.

The archbishop strengthened diplomatic relations

by becoming a personal friend of one of the great French cardinals. Eugene Cardinal Tisserant lived in Rome, as head of the Congregation of the Oriental Church, but he spent much time in Paris. And he never came to the French capital without spending many happy hours conversing with Roncalli at his home.

Engrossed as he was in diplomatic activities, the future pope never ceased his personal spiritual considerations. In France he wrote in his diary:

I must not disguise from myself the truth: I am definitely approaching old age. My mind resents this and almost rebels, for I still feel so young, eager, agile and alert. But one look in my mirror disillusions me. This is the season of maturity; I must do more and better, reflecting that perhaps the time still granted to me for living is brief, and that I am drawing to the gates of eternity. . . . This thought caused Hezekiah to turn to the wall and weep (2 Kings 20:2). I do not weep.

No, I do not weep, and I do not even desire to live my life over again, so as to do better. I entrust to the Lord's mercy whatever I have done, badly or less than well, and I look to the future, brief or long as it may be here below, because I want to make it holy and a source of holiness to others.

Archbishop Roncalli's work took him, by personal choice, into every corner of France. He came to know the country well, just as he had came to know Bulgaria, Turkey, and Greece. He traveled widely to learn about the people, their land, and their thoughts. Perhaps that is why his popularity was so great.

During his nine years in France, Roncalli visited eighty-five of the eighty-seven French dioceses. Before each visit, he studied the area, its history and current problems. During the visits he met priests, laymen, and town officials. He toured all the famous historical sites, as well as those which mark religious shrines. His favorite was still at Lourdes, which he had first visited with Bishop Radini-Tedeschi. Roncalli never failed to become emotionally moved in the presence of the Virgin Mary where Bernadette saw her. "Mary is always here," he said on his last visit there. ". . . always in the act of fulfilling her pious mission. She is here as she is in the grotto, the crypt, the upper and lower basilicas. She is always here, the Mother of Jesus. Always, she is here, ever in the act of carrying out her maternal mission, the mission proclaimed by her Son Jesus. She listens, enlightens, consoles, heals, and encourages all those who appeal to her."

Roncalli's longest trip as papal nuncio to France was to French North Africa in 1952. For thirty-eight days he toured Algeria, Morocco, and Tunisia.

Algeria was torn by internal strife over its relations with France. In a sermon to the Christians of Algeria, the archbishop preached, "My dear brethren, we should resist the voice of hate; we should remain faithful to love, peace and kindness. . . . My thoughts and my heart turn not only to our Catholic brethren but in the same way to all Christians of whatever persuasion who share with us Our Lord's message of love and to the great masses of many different races and tongues. . . ." He was for "unity in all necessary things, freedom in doubtful things, charity in all things." This, along with "obedience and peace," was one of his favorite maxims. His message of love and peace over war and misunderstanding was for thinking people everywhere, regardless of race or creed.

Angelo Roncalli hated war in every form. In 1940 he had said, "War is a frightful danger. For a Christian who believes in Jesus and His Gospel, it is an iniquity and a contradiction."

In 1952, as dean of the French diplomatic corps, he talked about war again: "Therefore, war is the ruin of civilization and the return to barbarism. Even when it is necessary to resist violence, when the defense of security and essential liberty makes such resistance inevitable, war must remain the last resort."

To this man, life was a holy gift, and that belief moved him to action whether it was among the starving Greeks or the captured Germans held in prison camps long after World War II had ended.

While in France, Roncalli was also appointed by the pope to become the Vatican observer to UNESCO (United Nations Educational, Scientific and Cultural Organization) with headquarters in Paris.

This post brought him in contact with people from all over the world who were as concerned as he about cultural and scientific matters. UNESCO is the largest branch of the UN, and nations who are not even members of the United Nations itself cooperate with it. Roncalli's ability to speak Bulgarian, Turkish, modern Greek, some Russian, Italian, and French made him a natural for such a post.

At first he was greatly concerned that UNESCO would have a tendency to teach one culture pattern in all needy nations and overlook the indigenous patterns of each area. But his fears were soon allayed and in a speech before the entire UNESCO assembly in 1951 he said, "UNESCO is no longer what one feared it might become, a big museum dedicated to diluting culture for the benefit of a curious throng. Instead it is a great, blazing fire whose sparks fly forth to arouse enthusiasm and cooperation on behalf of justice, freedom, and peace for all peoples without destruction of race, language or religion. . . ."

The opportunity to meet, plan, and exchange thoughts with UNESCO leaders no doubt enhanced his personal feelings on the oneness of mankind and its common need for cooperation and trust. It may have also further developed his personal ideas on the need for scientific and technological cooperation which filled an entire encyclical after he became pope.

On another occasion he said to UNESCO members, "We must live in the stream of history. . . . We who are approaching old age with our sack of experience

71

thrown over our shoulder, admit that there is much good will and a great confidence in the future among our contemporaries who are younger than we. Yes, we all want to be in the stream of history but not subjugated or turned upside down by it. . . ."

This kind of speech is typical of Roncalli throughout all his diplomatic ventures. He never became preachy over what people ought to be doing or thinking because "the Church says so." He spoke to man's good sense out of the wealth of his own good sense. He believed in man's good nature and appealed to his best judgment. Such an appeal was picked up by non-Catholic, non-Christian, and nonreligious people. His simplicity and optimism were contagious.

In December, 1952, Nuncio Roncalli received word from Rome that Pope Pius XII had appointed him a cardinal. The honor brought with it sadness, and he said, "Now I have to leave Paris. I have to leave France and all this is painful for me. . . ."

The official credentials were presented to him in a ceremony on January 15, 1953, by President Vincent Auriol, representing Pope Pius XII. The red hat of the cardinal was to be presented in Rome, by the pope. The dignitaries who were present included a Canadian, an Italian, a Turk, a Socialist, a Jew, a Calvinist, and a Moslem. They rejoiced over his honor and wept at their loss. He was praised for his paternal teachings, his efforts at peace, his love of the French people, and his constant aim for effective dialogue.

France gave him the Grand Cross of the Legion of

Honor and made him promise to return. He would do so twice.

Although the future pope's work in France would be overshadowed by his later elevation to the highest post in the church, his work with the French people was actually among his greatest achievements. He had done much to heal the scars left by years of war and German occupation and to soothe the animosity that the people felt toward the former government in Vichy.

On January 18, 1953, at the age of seventy-one, Cardinal Angelo Roncalli was named patriarch of Venice by Pope Pius XII. After thirty years, he was going back to Italy.

CHAPTER ELEVEN

RETURN TO ITALY

VENICE CELEBRATED! Perhaps never before or since had the city seen such a grand occasion as on March 15, 1953, when Cardinal Roncalli arrived as patriarch. Every building was decorated with colorful banners, gondolas were wreathed in flowers, beautiful tapestries hung from the bridges. The Grand Canal was filled with floating barges and gondolas. Over all, the bells from the carillon in St. Mark's Square could be heard. People were waving, shouting, and laughing.

Patriarch Roncalli wore bright scarlet robes, and he may have been the happiest person there. He waved to the throngs and smiled broadly over the beauty of this ancient city of his homeland. Down the Grand Canal went the procession of launches until they arrived at St. Mark's Square, where thousands of people greeted him with shouting and waving. He looked up at the old clock tower, built in 1496, and stepped into the nave of the Cathedral of St. Mark, second only to the Hagia Sophia, in Istanbul, as an example of Byzantine architecture.

74

Pope Pius XII with Cardinal Roncalli, then partriarch of Venice

As part of his speech in the cathedral that day he said, "The position confided to me in Venice is very great and far surpasses my merit. But I commend to your benevolence the man who wishes simply to be your brother, amiable, approachable, understandable . . . a man who wishes above all else to be your loving brother. Such is the man, such is the new citizen which Venice has been kind enough to welcome so festively today. . . ."

At seventy-one, Angelo Roncalli was beginning a new job. He felt wonderfully agile for a man of his years, but he was quite aware that old friends were dying. He was greatly saddened by the deaths of three of his sisters—two of them, Ancilla and Maria, had spent most of their lives keeping house for him. Instead of thinking about retirement he said, "I neither fear to die, nor refuse to live."

The cardinal continued the schedule he had always had—rise at 5 A.M., say Mass at 7, breakfast at 8. He reserved from 10 A.M. to 1 P.M. for callers, including the man on the street. Sometimes the crowd became a little too heavy, but when his secretary protested the patriarch said, "Let them come. They might want to confess."

Lunch was at 1, followed by a long prayer period, and then rest. At 7:45 P.M. he met his household staff to recite the rosary together. This was followed by dinner at 8. He retired at 10 P.M. Sometimes if he had to write a speech he would work until 4 A.M. and sleep until 7. His staff reported that once in a while he got up at 1 A.M. and prayed the rest of the night in his chapel.

Obviously, Angelo Roncalli was still a vigorous man. He never lost his temper and never appeared nervous or ill at ease. He maintained his calm and his sense of humor in every situation. This alone was a great accomplishment.

As a sidelight to his routine duties as patriarch, the future pope proclaimed certain rules about women's dress. Rumors of scanty bathing suits on Lido Beach in Venice brought forth a pronouncement about the immodesty of womanhood. On one occasion, when nine tourists wore short shorts in the Piazza San Marco, he protested, "I do not say that people need come to Italy in furs and woolens. They can come dressed in that modern American silk, fresh and soft, which is a veritable refrigerator at low cost. On the other hand Italy is not on the equator, and even there lions wear their fur coats, and crocodiles are protected by their expensive skins." He is also known to have prohibited tourists in sleeveless dresses from entering the Cathedral of St. Mark.

During his five years in Venice, Roncalli built a new minor seminary and a new building for housing patriarchal archives. He created thirty new parishes and reorganized some of the cathedral. The bodies of former patriarchs were brought to the cathedral for burial, the remains of Saint Mark were moved to beneath the high altar, precious relics were cleaned and put on public view, and Roncalli himself planned for his burial there.

In September, 1954, the cardinal was asked by Pope Pius XII to be papal legate to the Marian Congress in

Beirut, Lebanon. It was there that he met old friends of the Oriental branch of Christendom. Some of them believed, as deeply as Roncalli, that Orthodox reunion with Rome and other sects of Christianity must come. He earnestly prayed that the separated brethren might come into the fold "that all may be one."

Also in 1954, he celebrated the fiftieth anniversary of his ordination as a priest. On that day in 1904 Pope Pius X touched his head as a blessing in the main aisle at St. Peter's. Recalling that moment during a prayer to Saint Pius X in 1954, he prayed, "Oh Holy Father Pius X! On the day of my first Mass you stretched your hands over the head of the new priest kneeling as you passed by in the Vatican. I have always kept in my heart the memory of that gesture and the sweet words of well-wishing and benediction which accompanied it. Look down upon me now, fifty years after. . . ."

Yet, with all the honors which he had received, he was most proud of being a priest of humble origins. He never ceased loving the common people and feeling an identification with them.

On October 5, 1958, as he was receiving visitors, Patriarch Roncalli heard that eighty-two-year-old Eugenio Pacelli, Pope Pius XII, had suffered a stroke. Immediately the cardinal retired to his chapel and spent the next three days praying for the man whom he had first known as a vibrant lecturer at the seminary in Rome.

Early on October 9 word came that the pope was dead.

Roncalli's first duty was to celebrate high requiem

mass in the Cathedral of St. Mark. His second duty was to pack for the conclave of cardinals in Rome, which would elect a successor.

In the Catholic Church, the office of cardinal is second only to that of the pope. Together, the cardinals make up the papal senate, or college of cardinals. The number of cardinals in the college has varied. In the sixteenth century, it was fixed at not more than seventy, but today there is no limit on membership in the college. One of its chief duties is to elect a new pope, for which purpose the college must meet in Rome not more than eighteen days after the former pope's death.

According to Cardinal Roncalli's secretary, Monsignor Loris Capovilla, the cardinal packed his red cape, which would be worn to pay his respects to the newly elected pope, but in his haste he did not even pack personal books or papers for the train ride to Rome.

On October 12, the stationmaster, Vittorio de Rosa, escorted the patriarch to his seat on the train. Roncalli said, "The other day, immediately after the Pontifical Mass for the exequies of the Pope, I wanted to tell you something, but there were so many people and I had no opportunity. . . . I will speak of it to you when I return."

The stationmaster replied, "It is my good wish for you, your eminence, that you will not return."

As if lost in thought, Cardinal Roncalli finally said, "My hope is to return to Venice within fifteen days."

CHAPTER TWELVE

"WE HAVE A POPE"

ROME WAS IN MOURNING. Black drapes covered doors, windows, and arches. Behind them lay a city in sorrow. Bells tolled, newspapers were edged in black, and solemn rites filled the next nine days.

In the sweltering October heat, the body of Eugenio Pacelli, Pope Pius XII, was borne from Castel Gandolfo, outside Rome, toward St. Peter's Basilica. Thousands of people lined the streets and knelt as the glass-walled hearse passed by. The route wound by the Colosseum, the Arch of Constantine, beside the Roman Forum, and finally to St. Peter's Square. Drums rolled and the clergy chanted prayers. When the hearse reached the stately colonnade at St. Peter's, the great bells of the church began to toll. It was estimated that 300,000 people filled the square and watched in silence. Swiss Guards of the Vatican met the hearse and directed it through the crowds. The immense doors of the church opened and the body was carried into the nave and placed on a bier.

For four days, great numbers of people filled the

church in sorrow and respect. On the fourth night Pope Pius XII was buried near the tomb of Saint Peter in the Vatican Grotto.

The college of cardinals, led by Dean Cardinal Tisserant, wore purple instead of scarlet. For the next nine days, the papal apartment in the Vatican was sealed. The college of cardinals would technically govern the Church until a new pope was chosen.

Cardinals who were unable to make diplomatic arrangements to leave their posts behind the Iron Curtain by the funeral date hoped to do so by the opening of the conclave on Saturday, October 25.

By October 16, forty-five of the fifty-five members of the college of cardinals were in Rome. Finally, Stefan Cardinal Wyszinski, archbishop at Warsaw, was granted leave from Poland. Cardinal Stepinac of Yugoslavia was too ill to make the trip, but Cardinal Mindszenty of Hungary still clung to the hope that he would be allowed to leave his country. The United States Department of State intervened in his behalf, but Hungary refused to grant permission. When October 25 arrived, fifty-three cardinals made up the college of cardinals. On the morning of the twenty-sixth Cardinal Costantini of Armenia died suddenly, lowering the total to fifty-two.

As the day came near for the conclave to convene, Rome became a city of excited rumors. As in any election every man on the street had his favorite candidate. Newspapers all over the world were publishing pictures and histories of the possible choices.

Cardinal Roncalli (second row, with eyes closed) joins other cardinals to elect a new pope, October, 1958.

Following Cardinal Roncalli's name, some papers added: "He is the candidate of the French Cardinals: Roncalli, if elected, will call himself Pius XIII." Another paper said: "Roncalli is the most probable because he has never shown any very definite leaning toward groups. He is acquainted with the problems of international affairs. . . ."

During the nine days of mourning for Pius XII, Cardinal Roncalli stayed in the large brick building which houses the headquarters of Women's Catholic Action in Rome. His personal secretary, Capovilla, was with him. The building was within a ten-minute ride to the Vatican.

Between masses and ceremonies for the dead pope, the cardinal toured his favorite haunts in Rome. He visited the Church of Santa Maria, where he had been ordained a priest fifty-four years before, and the altar in St. Peter's where he had said his first mass. He visited the church where he had been consecrated a bishop and the grave of Cesare Cardinal Baronius, whose motto, *"Obedientia et pax,"* he had adopted for his own.

Of course, he must have been aware that he was a contender for the papacy. His record was good. He had worked well at his many posts. He was not too conservative or too liberal, but neither was he a fence-sitter. More than being political, he was a pastoral priest.

There was talk of electing an "interim" pope—one

who would quietly fill the post until a stronger, more forceful candidate could be found.

On Saturday, October 25, 1958, the college of cardinals, once more clad in scarlet robes, entered St. Peter's for a Votive Mass of the Holy Spirit. They heard a sermon by Monsignor Bacci who said, ". . . We have need of a pontiff with a great strength of mind and ardent charity; a pontiff who knows how to tell the truth even to those who do not wish to hear it; who knows how to defend the rights of Christian and human civilization, but at the same time to open the arms of pardon to all. . . . He must be a teacher . . . and a pastor . . . but also a father. . . . May the new Vicar of Christ be like a bridge between heaven and earth . . . may he be like a bridge between social classes . . . finally may he be like a bridge between nations, even among those who reject, repel, and persecute the Christian religion. . . ."

Following the mass each cardinal returned to his room, packed his belongings, and moved into the Vatican for the official conclave. Even while preparations were in progress to bury Pope Pius XII, rooms were being readied around the Sistine Chapel to shut the college of cardinals away from the eyes of the world until after the election.

Each cardinal was allowed one aide to assist him during the conclave, and Roncalli invited his secretary to enter confinement with him.

A temporary brick wall sealed off the cardinals from the outside. One single door, locked from both sides, could be used in emergency. Six revolving panels allowed food and other supplies to be swung inside the sealed-off area. The windows were whitewashed, telephones disconnected, and radios ruled out. Complete secrecy reigned over the college of cardinals as they prayed, discussed, and voted for a new pope.

As the cardinals were moving into the Vatican, and crowds gathered outside to maintain their vigilance, Cardinal Mooney of Detroit died of a heart attack. He had attended the Votive Mass and had died that afternoon. His death brought the voting delegates to fifty-one.

So, on October 25, 1958, fifty-one cardinals of the Roman Catholic Church were sealed into secrecy around the Sistine Chapel. In the presence of their aides, the cardinals took an oath that they would, not discuss the official proceedings—either with each other or the outside world. Then the aides took an oath to abide by the same rules.

Chairs and writing desks for each cardinal were arranged around the chapel. Above each chair was a purple canopy. In one corner was a black iron stove with a long stovepipe reaching to the high window. The ballots are burned in this stove following each session. If no one is elected pope, the ballots are burned with straw to create black smoke. When a pope is chosen, the ballots are burned without straw to create white smoke. Either way the vigilant crowds outside know something of the proceedings as they watch the stovepipe sticking out from the window.

85

During the next three days, the cardinals voted twice each morning and twice each afternoon. The ballots are printed in Latin with the words, "I elect as Supreme Pontiff the most reverend Lord Cardinal ————." Each ballot is sealed with wax, and the cardinals disguise their handwriting to augment secrecy.

The ballots are not collected. Each cardinal comes forward, kneels in prayer before the altar, and lays his ballot on the altar. The altar is covered with a green cloth which holds a silver chalice. As he stands before the altar the cardinal says, "The Lord Christ, who shall be my judge, is witness that I choose the one whom I believe should be chosen according to God."

To elect a pope, the vote must be two thirds plus one of the cardinals. Each time the fifty-one cardinals voted, those who were chosen to be tellers counted the ballots, opened them, called each name aloud, and tallied their sheets. The ballots were mixed with straw and burned in the stove. The signal of black smoke disappointed half a million people in St. Peter's Square.

As in most elections, probably some candidates were tied, some pulled ahead at first and then slowly lost ground. The details of what actually takes place are never revealed.

Black smoke continued to pour from the chimney, producing more rumor and speculation. The crowds grew, and pressed more tightly against each other, all eyes on the smokestack.

By the third morning the cardinals must surely have

been tired. But from certain statements spoken after-
ward by Pope John, we know that the tension broke on
that morning.

"I knew by certain signs that I would be chosen," he
said. By watching the voting results, he knew, no
doubt, which candidates pulled ahead, and which fell
back not to be considered again. His reaction was fear
over the terrible burden of responsibility. It seems that
he really did not want to be elected. His first choice
was to return to Venice as he had promised the stationmaster.

Following the morning balloting, the cardinals returned to their quarters for lunch. Cardinal Roncalli
spent the time in prayer, preparing for what he felt
was coming. The time passed quickly.

The cardinals were called for the eleventh ballot.
When all the votes had been read, Cardinals Tisserant,
Ran Roey, and Canali walked to the chair where
Cardinal Roncalli was seated. In Latin, Cardinal
Tisserant, as dean of the college of cardinals, said, "Do
you accept your election, made canonically, as Supreme Pontiff?" It was the most important question
that Angelo Roncalli had ever faced. He would be
allowed to say no. If he said yes, it would mean grave
responsibility for this seventy-seven-year-old man. It
would mean taking on great burdens at a time when
most men are ready to retire.

"I tremble and am afraid. My poorness and little-
ness fills me with confusion. But I see in the votes of
my eminent brother cardinals the sign of the will of

God. Therefore, I accept the election. I bow my head and bend my back to the yoke of the cross."

When he had finished speaking, he looked up and saw fifty canopies being lowered. Only his remained. He knew he was the pope.

"By what name shall you be called?" asked Cardinal Tisserant.

"I shall be called John," the new pope answered.

His choice probably sent an audible reaction through the gathered crowd when they heard it. Like the news media, they may have assumed that the new pope would call himself Pius XIII. No one had chosen the name John for 550 years.

The new pope said, "This name is sweet to us, because it is the name of our father. It is sweet to us because it is the name of the humble parish church in which we were baptized; it is the name of innumerable cathedrals . . . and first of all the sacred Lateran Basilica, our cathedral [as Bishop of Rome]. It is the name which has been borne by the most popes in the long list of Roman pontiffs; in fact, there are twenty-two supreme pontiffs of undoubted legitimacy with the name of John. Virtually all of them had short pontificates. We have preferred to cover the smallness of our name behind the magnificent succession of Roman pontiffs."

He also said that Saint Mark, patron of Venice, was called by the name John. It was the name of John the Baptist and John the Evangelist. "May God graciously grant, Venerable Brothers, that we . . . by the aid of divine grace have the same holiness of life and strength of soul that we may, if God wills, even be prepared to shed our blood."

When he had finished speaking, the secretary of the Conclave, Alberto di Jorio, offered him the white skullcap. The new pope took off his scarlet hat, placed it on the head of di Jorio, showing that the secretary would become a cardinal, and walked to the main altar for prayer.

He was then led to the sacristy of the Sistine Chapel, and was dressed in white preparatory to his first public appearance before the crowds outside. By this time the people had seen the white smoke, but they did not know the new pope's name.

To make sure that the white robes would fit any one of the cardinals who might be elected, the Vatican tailor made up three sets in different sizes. He figured that any cardinal would fit into one of them. But he did not count on the width of Pope John who later admitted, "I felt all tied up."

During the robing, Monsignor Capovilla assisted the new pope. Then, dressed in white, Pope John returned to the Sistine Chapel where he gave his first blessing to the kneeling cardinals from a throne that had been brought into the church. It was here that Pope John took his first step away from the traditional. As each cardinal kneels and kisses the pope's hand, it is traditional that they also kiss his foot. But Pope John refused to allow this, and instead he embraced each one with a kiss of peace.

Surely the wild cries of the excited people outside could be heard in the chapel. They called, "We have a pope. Long live the pope!"

At 6 P.M. officials filed onto the balcony above St. Peter's Square. Cardinal Canali, dean of the cardinal deacons, stepped to the microphone and said, "I bring you joyful news. We have a pope! He is the eminent Lord Cardinal Angelo Guiseppe Roncalli who has taken the name of Pope John XXIII."

Amid happy cheers and the booming of bells, Pope John appeared. He raised his hand, giving in Latin his first blessing *Urbi et Orbi* [to the city and to the world]: "Blessed be the name of the Lord! Now and also forever! Our help is in the name of the Lord! Who made heaven and earth! May you be blessed by Almighty God, the Father and the Son and the Holy Spirit!"

The crowds lingered far into the night. Inside the Vatican, the pope's apartment was being readied, repairmen were putting back telephones, and everyone was bringing back to life an area which had been sealed off for three days.

At 10 P.M. Pope John read his first public message over Italian radio. It was translated into thirty-six languages for rebroadcasting.

The message, emphasizing unity, forgiveness, and peace, included:

In a special way our thoughts go to the bishops, priests, sisters, and all the faithful who dwell in

Pope John XXIII blesses the crowd after his elevation to the papacy.

those nations . . . where men dare to trample the sacred rights of the Church. . . . We wish them all to know that we share their sorrows, hardships and distress and that we beg God, the giver of all good things, that some day He may put an end to such human persecution. . . . May He enlighten the minds of the rulers of these nations with His divine light. May He grant pardon to Persecutors. May all enjoy lawful freedom most speedily and may He bestow on them better and happier times . . . and to all who are separated from this Apostolic See . . . to these we open our heart most lovingly and extend open arms. Ardently desiring their return to the house of the common Father . . . we pray that all may come willingly and gladly. . . . No strange house will they find, but their own.

Few people knew what vigor this elderly man had. If they thought of him as an old, worn-out interim pope before an active one might be found, they were wrong. He had vigor, health, and, above all, a marvelous sense of humor. No one could guess how exciting the Vatican would become during the reign of Pope John XXIII.

CHAPTER THIRTEEN

GOOD POPE JOHN

FROM THE BEGINNING, Pope John XXIII had a style of his own. He was not a theologian eager to make new statements on doctrine. In fact, he once said (referring to theologians): "They are the ones who got us into our present-day difficulties. It's up to ordinary Christians like you and me to extricate ourselves from them."

Historically, it was the right of every pope to endow his relatives with princely titles and even to allow them to live in the Vatican rent free. Pope John broke tradition again when he said that his brothers and nephews would be called "brothers and nephews of the pope." It was as easy as that. He added, "I believe that should be enough. And it seems to me that since they have expressed the wish to remain in their poor homes in Sotto il Monte, this is their greatest nobility."

Pope John was not a genius scholastically, theologically, or philosophically. He was a gentle man with tremendous dedication to a mighty task. He loved people, which was perhaps his greatest virtue. In lov-

93

ing people he was sensitive to their needs, their weaknesses, and their inner and outer disciplines.

His own informality drew people to him. Traditionally, the gardeners had to leave the Vatican when the pope wanted to meditate. Pope John insisted they stay so he could watch them and talk with them.

Traditionally, the pope ate alone in silence. Pope John lasted only a few days in this seclusion. He said, "I value tradition and I grant that my predecessors did, too. I must confess, however, that I have never found any place in the Bible which suggests that the pope must eat alone." He invited his secretary, Capovilla, to eat with him from then on.

Traditionally, popes seldom ventured alone from the Vatican. But this was too much for Pope John and it did not take him long to go out when no one was looking. Often, his associates had no idea where he was and they would rush about, frantically looking for him. Finally, they persuaded him to stop his wanderings in the streets of Rome.

It was difficult for the Pope to see the importance of the sedan chair in which a pope is carried through crowds. "The motion makes me dizzy," he said. The expensive chair is carried on the shoulders of twelve men, and it looks like an elaborate throne. Only after much persuasion did he admit that people could see him better if he was carried in the chair.

By custom, popes are expected to use the official "we" in official statements. This, too, was difficult for him. "I" slipped in more often than not, which made him even more endearing to people. Vatican protocol was not easy to learn overnight by a man who had been humble all his life.

Pope John visited the churches of Rome, as well as the orphanages, jails, and people along the streets. He talked with anyone and everyone. It was a part of his charm and his loving acceptance of people as children of God. Whatever their political party, their occupation, or station in life, Pope John loved individual people.

According to a story, one of Italy's best-known Communists was clapping and shouting one day with approval for Pope John. When asked why he was yelling so loudly, he answered: "He [the Pope] is the son of a worker. He knows what manual labor is. I'm clapping for a poor man of the people who has been made pope."

Shortly after becoming pope, John XXIII visited the prison Regina Coeli. No one could remember when a pope had ever visited a prison. While he was there he not only told the prisoners about one of his relatives who was caught for poaching, but he said, "When I was a boy I stole something once; it was an apple. My feelings of remorse were just as great as yours, and for a long time I repented for my sin. But I was lucky; I was not caught! How could I have given the apple back anyway? I had eaten it a long time ago!"

On November 4, 1958, this man was officially crowned as the 259th person to succeed Peter the Apostle as head of the Roman Catholic Church.

What does this actually mean? To understand the significance of Pope John XXIII, we must understand the significance of being a pope. In reality, to follow the long line of popes is to follow the history of the Roman Catholic Church.

The pope is the ruler of the Church. The title was first mentioned by Saint Ennodius and used generally since the eleventh century. The pope is considered to be a direct successor to Peter, the fisherman, the disciple, the Apostle of Jesus Christ.

Scripturally, the pope's authority begins in the Gospel of Saint Matthew, Chapter 16, Verse 18, with Jesus' commission to Peter:

"And I do say to thee, Thou art Peter, and upon this rock I will build my church, and the gates of hell shall not prevail against it."

Another time Jesus asked Peter to take care of his flock and to feed his sheep, as if placing special responsibility upon Peter.

Peter was a leader by nature, and it was not always easy for him to be a patient follower. Sometimes he was impetuous. But above all he was loyal and responsive. After the death of Jesus, Christian groups scattered throughout Asia Minor—Jerusalem, Galilee, Samaria, Corinth, Philippi, Thessalonica, Rome, and other places. Peter was looked upon as their leader. He had personally organized the Christians and was finally martyred after his imprisonment.

When Peter died in 42 A.D., his authority was continuously passed to someone else, until Pope John was given the responsibility over nineteen hundred years later.

A pope is referred to as "Servant of the Servants of God," but his full title is "Bishop of Rome, Vicar of Jesus Christ, Successor of the Prince of the Apostles, Supreme Pontiff of the Universal Church, Patriarch of the West, Primate of Italy, Archbishop and Metropolitan of the Roman Province, and Sovereign of the State of Vatican City."

Technically, any Roman Catholic can be elected pope but in actuality the pope is chosen from among the college of cardinals, known also as the sacred college. Their most important duty is the election of a new pope.

Ten important facts about the papacy are:

1. The pope is the vicar of Jesus Christ on earth.
2. The pope is the bishop of Rome and, as head of the Church of Rome, he is head of the whole Catholic Church.
3. He is the head of the Catholic Apostolic and Roman Church with its 472 million members spread over five continents.
4. He is head of the Catholic clergy, from its seventy-five cardinals to its million nuns.
5. The pope is guardian of the Catholic faith, the sacred traditions, and the books handed from generation to generation.

6. The pope is supreme doctor of the church. When he speaks concerning faith or morals, his statements carry that authority.

7. The pope is sovereign. Nations recognize his state of the Vatican City.

8. The pope is heir of the Roman pontiffs, which covers both the Roman Empire and the Christian Era.

9. The pope (or papacy) is the meeting place where current spiritual trends are sorted out and fused.

10. The pope is the keystone at the apex of a vast Catholic world structure.

The coronation day of a pope is one of the most colorful spectaculars in Catholic tradition. It is a time of processions, choruses, and a four-hour ceremony. Trumpets, bells, and cheers of "Long live the Pope!" make it an occasion to be remembered.

Amid mitered patriarchs and cardinals, Pope John was carried in his swaying throne on the shoulders of twelve men. As he entered the nave of the cathedral and neared the altar, it was obvious that he was looking for someone. Finally, his face broke into a radiant smile as he caught the eyes of his brothers and sisters, and gave them a special blessing.

Precedent was broken in two ways during the coronation ceremony. First, powerful lights were allowed so that everyone might see. In fact, during a quiet moment one of the overheated lights exploded.

Pope John XXIII receives the three-tiered crown of gold, silver, and diamonds.

The coronation of Pope John XXIII, November 4, 1958

Second, Pope John spoke unexpectedly from his throne. His text concerned the divisions in Christianity, and his desire for the separated brothers to come into the fold "that all may be one."

The crowning ceremony took four minutes. Cardinal Tisserant prayed the Lord's Prayer and the Coronation Prayer. Cardinal Ottaviani lifted off the tall golden miter from the pope's head. Cardinal Canali raised the great triple tiara, set with jewels, and placed it on the lowered head of Pope John XXIII, saying, "Receive the tiara adorned with three crowns and know that you are the Father of princes and of kings, Pontiff of the whole world and Vicar on Earth of Our Lord Jesus Christ to whom be honor and glory for ever and ever!"

The crowds shouted in joy, *"Viva il Papa!"* and Pope John later blessed them from the balcony of St. Peter's.

This was the beginning of a five-year papal reign that changed the face of the Vatican and the position of the pope in the world.

CHAPTER FOURTEEN

THE NEW LOOK

THE VATICAN took on a new look. Pope John was a man who cracked jokes, took walks on the streets of Rome, and talked with everyone. He smiled easily and was constantly on the move. Everyone loved him.

"It's incredible," said a policeman assigned on escort duty, "you just can't stop this pope. He's constantly on the move. I never have a peaceful minute any more. My spaghetti is always cold when I get home."

The rush of activities kept Rome's press busy. In one day Pope John appointed twenty-three new cardinals and made Domenico Tardini not only a new cardinal but secretary of state for the Vatican. This move raised the college of cardinals from seventy to seventy-five for the first time in four hundred years.

Although most popes had been prisoners of the Vatican, trips around Rome became a usual pattern for Pope John. He was a pastor. As bishop of Rome he had a flock all his own—thousands of the faithful who needed him as he needed them. He preached to the students who were becoming priests at the Pontifical Gregorian University; he visited Rome's Gesu Bambino Hospital for Children, as well as the jails, Santo Spirito Hospital for Adults, the orphanage of Villa Nazareth, and crippled children in the Don Gnocchi Home. He talked with all kinds of people, showing his love, his concern, and sometimes his sorrow for their conditions. At the crippled children's home he said, "Tears, sorrow, and sufferings of men must not be wasted, because they have a purpose."

He was aware of the tremendous poverty in Rome. People living in shacks depressed him, and he referred to them as, "My personal mission territory."

One other innovation worth noting is that he had a movie theatre built into the Vatican, and for the first time in over two hundred years a pope watched a dramatic performance. His first viewing was of T. S. Eliot's *Murder in the Cathedral*. He enjoyed it greatly.

The greatest impetus to the new look came less than three months after his election to the papacy. On January 25, 1959, Pope John was visiting the church of Saint Paul-Outside-the-Walls. In a speech that day he took the Catholic Church by surprise when he called for an ecumenical council. He wanted to update the Church and make it more relevant to the age it served. He also called for Christian unity among those branches of the separated brethren who had long before pulled away from Rome.

Speaking to the Benedictine monks of Saint Paul's, he said, "The new pope hopes to bring to the attention of the whole world the ancient truth reflected under new forms. Some people dare to speak ill of the Church, claiming it is behind the times. But the Church is alive and is not the custodian of a museum. Though the Church has a great respect for what is ancient, beautiful and good, her first concern is souls. . . ."

He announced the coming of three events of great importance: a diocesan synod (advisory body) for the city of Rome, celebration of an ecumenical (all churches) council for the Universal Church, and the updating of the code of canon law.

The reaction was spontaneous. Dr. Visser't Hooft of the World Council of Churches said that Pope John's plan for the ecumenical council demonstrated "the tremendous importance which the problem of unity has assumed in our times." The Orthodox Metropolitan Antony Bashir said, "I do not find any reason why the apostolic churches should be divided. There is only one holy Apostolic Church. Its differences could be ironed out in ecumenical councils. . . ."

The name Vatican II began to be heard. What did it mean, and what was Vatican I? To those outside the Roman Catholic Church, the terms were meaningless, but words like "unity," or "the Church is alive and is not the custodian of a museum" struck home.

In succeeding days Pope John spoke over and over of his hopes for the council. Dates were set, committees got underway, and commissions were established.

Cardinal Tardini headed the preparatory commission, whose organization was massive. It had been almost one hundred years since such a council had met, and the event demanded powerful competence. Cardinal Montini of Milan believed the council to be "the greatest which the Church has ever celebrated in its twenty centuries of history." It is said that one clergyman told the pope that it would be absolutely impossible to open the council in 1963. "Fine, we'll open it in 1962!" said Pope John.

And, indeed, the pope announced that Vatican II would begin on October 11, 1962. He felt this would grant ample time for the commissions to study every area in which the Church served and to submit their reports, questions, and problems to the central commission making up the agenda for the council.

By the opening date Pope John would be eighty years old. Instead of a tottering old man ready for retirement, he was full of vigor and excitement. Whether or not he ever realized what his announcement of the council would instigate, the whole idea was in keeping with his entire lifework. He believed in unity. He believed in the power and mission of the Church. He believed that the Church must not only exist in the world; it must speak, act, and make an impact. Vatican II offered him the perfect platform from which "to open the windows of the Church to fresh air."

The first Vatican council had been held under Pope

Pius IX in 1870. In entire church history, only twenty ecumenical councils had ever been called, and their purpose had been to meet some particular crisis.

Pope John saw the church as one great family and in Vatican II he gave the impression of a father calling for a family reunion.

Unity was a key word now. Anglicans, other Protestants, and some Greek Orthodox churches were especially outspoken affirming Pope John's desire for greater togetherness. Some cardinals felt that the pope was too optimistic. On the opening day of the council he spoke frankly about pessimism in the ranks, saying, "In the daily exercise of Our pastoral office Our ears are shocked, much to Our regret, by the voices of persons who, though burning with religious zeal, are not endowed with too much sense of discretion and measure. In these modern times they can see nothing but calamities and ruin. They say that our era, in comparison with past eras, is getting worse, and they behave as though they have learned nothing from history, which is the teacher of life. . . . We feel we must declare our total disagreement with these prophets of doom who always foretell catastrophes as though the world were close to its end."

Through all the preparatory months, when he was asked what he expected from the council, Pope John would reply, "I expect a little fresh air!" His favorite motto for the council was: "Stress that which unites rather than that which divides."

"We do not intend to conduct a trial of the past. We

do not want to prove who was right or who was wrong. All we want to say is, 'Let us come together; let us make an end of our division.'"

John appointed Cardinal Bea, a brilliant theologian and confessor to Pius XII, as chairman of the council's secretariat for the union of Christians. He reminded him, "In working for reunion it is necessary first to be very humble; second, to be patient and await God's hour; and third, to avoid any discussions that may impair the virtue of charity. We must leave aside, for the moment, those elements on which we differ."

Pope John was interested not only in reaching Protestants and Orthodox who had broken away from Rome but he saw great room for improvement between Catholicism and Judaism; and even between those who call themselves atheists.

Two special events during these days were visits from United States President Dwight Eisenhower and Geoffrey Fisher, the Archbishop of Canterbury. Both were Protestants in highly esteemed positions. A few years before, their visits would have been frowned upon by clergy and laity. But so great was the universal acceptance of Pope John that, except for a few grumbles, these audiences were accepted. In 1963 Pope John granted an audience to Aleksei Adzhubei, editor of the Soviet newspaper *Izvestia*, son-in-law to Nikita Khrushchev, then premier of the Soviet Union. The pope broke all tradition in 1961 by appointing four Catholic observers to the Third Assembly of the World Council of Christians held in New Delhi, India.

It was little publicized, but an event of great importance in the light of Vatican change occurred on November 19, 1960, when Pope John presided over a Mass of the Catholic Eastern Rite in St. Peter's. Prayers were said in the Old Slavonic language. It was the first time in over one thousand years that such a service had been allowed in St. Peter's at all, let alone with a pope conducting it.

"We expect great things of the council," John kept reiterating. His optimism held. "There is an uncertainty, you might even say a holy commotion, that goes with starting something new, and this in itself is an exercise in humility. But all this is soon transformed into a courageous feeling of confidence as each new ray of light makes the horizon grow brighter and gradually reveals the Lord's Hand intervening to enlighten us, and to encourage us to move ahead with a generous heart and a willing spirit."

The preparatory commission, under Cardinal Tardini, began preliminary work by sending questionnaires to over 3,500 bishops, heads of orders in the Catholic Church, and Catholic universities to establish the council agenda. Their immediate replies showed the urgency and interest in updating the Church. "They have sent us enough for ten councils!" one archbishop said.

Preparations were made to have 3,500 delegates at the council. The physical arrangements alone were of momentous proportions. Cardinals, patriarchs, primates, abbots, archbishops, and bishops were to be voting delegates. Theologians and canonists were invited for consultation, and thirty-five official observers representing seventeen organizations and churches were also included, but they would not participate in debate. Most Eastern Orthodox did not participate, but two observers came from the patriarchate of Moscow after the council was underway. All voting was tabulated electronically, and speeches in debates were limited to ten minutes.

Rome was getting ready for company. The influx of summer tourists was one thing, but ten thousand people staying for several months was something else again. Hotels, restaurants, and the city in general contemplated the events. The news media wired St. Peter's Cathedral as well as every major street.

Pope John kept a guiding hand on every important area of preparatory work. The central committee, composed of fifty-eight cardinals, was directly under his leadership as chairman.

For three and one-half years, Pope John made clarifying speeches to define, redefine, guide, and inform as to the council purposes. In his Christmas, 1961, address, he said, "We gave them the arduous task of suggesting outlines for decrees concerning faith and morals from among which we would choose the ones to be taken up in the general sessions of the Council. It gives us great joy to tell you that these preparations . . . to which cardinals, bishops, prelates, theologians, canon lawyers, and learned men have contributed their distinguished cooperative efforts are on the verge of being completed. . . ."

His joy was obvious. His steps toward change had been accepted and welcomed. The only sadness in his heart was the sudden death of Cardinal Tardini in June, 1961.

CHAPTER FIFTEEN

DEFINING THE DREAM

POPE JOHN gave the world a touch of the Good Shepherd. By doing so, he earned a father image with humanity as well as with his own flock. He pointed up mutual goals, our single attachment to life, and our binding responsibility to improve the world. He believed that his Church should be a positive influence and that inner renewal would ignite outer vitality.

From 1959 to 1963 Pope John issued several encyclicals (letters), which defined his dreams for the ecumenical council. Three of these were of major significance, for they established the breadth of his thinking in the minds of men.

The first encyclical came on June 29, 1959, and was entitled *Ad Petri Cathedram* (meaning "from the chair of Saint Peter," or as pope rather than as an individual Catholic). It is significant because some of the cardinals were changing their minds about the worth of having a council. "The chief end of the Council," the encyclical states, "is to advance the growth of the Catholic faith; the renewal of Christian life among the people; and the adaptation of Church discipline to the needs and conditions of our time. This event will furnish a wonderful spectacle of truth, unity and charity. . . ."

This meant that the fresh air or the *aggiornamento* (updating) of which the pope spoke would be related to Catholic liturgy, canon law, and theology. Yet close to his heart was a dream much greater than theology or liturgy.

In *Ad Petri Cathedram*, he went into areas beyond the spiritual; those of the obligations of the press to truthfulness, the moral obligations of radio, television, and motion pictures. He spoke about brotherhood, agreements between nations, social classes, the duties of employers, and the responsibilities of employees. The last section was on the unity of the Church which continued to be one of his main objectives for the council.

In addition to this, he dealt with "the seeking and promoting, under the impulse of charity, of truth, of unity and peace."

One author said, "In the section of unity, harmony, and peace, Pope John wrote wisely and profoundly on subjects as the brotherhood of all men; union and agreement between nations; union and agreement between social classes; the problems of labor, stressing the duty of employers 'to provide in some suitable way for workers to share more and more in the fruits of labor and feel themselves partners in the whole enterprise' and on unity within the family."

The second great encyclical, issued on May 15,

1961, was entitled *Mater et Magistra* (Mother and Teacher). The opening sentence of this encyclical speaks of the Catholic Church as the "Mother and Teacher of all nations."

This letter was issued in commemoration of the seventieth anniversary of the famous encyclical *Rerum Novarum* (of revolutionary change) of Leo XIII. In *Mater et Magistra* Pope John dwelt on the position of the Church toward working people. His words give dignity to individuals and demand that all working people of every class benefit by modern technology. (Early in his reign, John became aware of the low salary scale of Vatican employees and he immediately rectified it. The salaries of gardeners, cooks, and all those who worked at such tasks in the Vatican were raised by 15 percent. Later he included the clergy up through cardinals.) Pope John knew what it was to work in the fields. He knew that most farmers, for example, lacked both the dignity of their labor and the benefits of technology. Included in the encyclical is the assertion that wealthy nations have a responsibility toward underdeveloped nations.

Mater et Magistra actually deals with four main problems: the depressed state of agriculture in an ever-increasing industrial world; the massive differences between underdeveloped nations and technologically developed nations; the increase in world population and its relationship to economic development; and the lack of mutual trust among nations.

In this encyclical he said, "These problems must be solved in terms of truth, justice, and love." He drew a sharp distinction between socialism and socialization, condemning the first and encouraging the second.

At one point he said that the shift of country people to the city is not necessarily a good thing. The lure of more money and better living conditions seem to be at the base of it, but on the other hand the travelers may be exchanging one kind of poverty for another. City living does not mean better living conditions. Perhaps, he said, the solution is to improve living conditions in the country.

". . . considerable thought must be given, especially by public authorities, to the suitable development of essential public services in country areas: roads, transport, means of communication, drinking water, housing, health services, elementary, technical and professional education, religious and recreational facilities, and the supply of modern installations and furnishings for the farm residence. . . ."

The encyclical speaks of taxation, credit banks, social insurance, promotion of industries, and price protection. In other words, the pope felt that farmers received unfair treatment and that modern economists must work at schemes to help improve the rural standard of living.

The entire encyclical is a masterpiece of social teaching. If it had been issued by an economist or a government it would still be good. But the fact that it was issued by a pastor makes it doubly noteworthy. For Pope John XXIII was surely helping the Church to see something of its responsibility in the modern era.

He wanted the Church to take the leadership in serving the total life of man, not just his spiritual needs.

The third encyclical, *Pacem in Terris,* issued April 12, 1963, overshadowed every other pronouncement from Pope John. From the first sentence it was special. Addressed "to all men of goodwill" rather than only to Catholics, it set forth a new statement on the rights of man. Some people compare it with the Magna Charta, the Bill of Rights, and other great statements in history.

Men of goodwill from every nation and every religion have praised this twenty-two-thousand-word document. It called for international peace, disarmament, a nuclear-test ban, better relations with the Communist world, guarantees of the rights of minorities, and freedom.

Again, its author was universally acclaimed as "good Pope John," and praised for his role as father and pastor of the world community.

Pacem in Terris broke tradition when it recognized the rights of a man "to worship God in accordance with the right dictates of his own conscience, and to profess his religion both in private and in public. . . ."

John left room for the differences in men. He erased the common mold which tradition required of everyone. "Truth calls for the elimination of every trace of racial discrimination . . . as we know from experience, men frequently differ widely in knowledge, virtue, intelligence and wealth, but the fact is that no one can be by nature superior to his fellows, since all men are equally noble in natural dignity. . . ."

As one statement read:

Pacem in Terris is far more than a noble preachment. It does not simply summon us to a crusade against war; it challenges us to plan and execute a detailed and comprehensive campaign against war's root causes. Among much else, it urges us to deploy the world's great store of physical resources and human resourcefulness in an attack against hunger and ignorance, disease, and destitution. It calls on us to use science and technology for meeting our vast human needs rather than for menacing each other with vast, and utterly inhuman, destruction. It asks each man to combat bigotry, unreason, and narrow partisanship, and bids each to begin this difficult fight within his own heart. Finally, *Pacem in Terris* clearly implies that all men in all nations, whatever their professional or private responsibilities, must accept a measure of personal responsibility for action.

In short, Pope John has confronted us with a choice we cannot avoid—a choice between toil and sweat for peace, or blood and tears in war.

This encyclical was issued after the first session of Vatican II. Perhaps John, too, had been spurred on by the expansive thinking of council delegates. *Pacem in Terris* stands as a great inspiration, beside that of the council itself.

CHAPTER SIXTEEN

THE COUNCIL OPENS

"NOBODY AROUND HERE knows how to run an ecumenical council. After all none of us have ever been to one," said Pope John to a group of bishops from Pakistan.

Nevertheless, the council opened on October 11, 1962, and the first session lasted until December 8.

Opening day was one of the greatest spectacles ever seen in Rome. Nothing was omitted—drama, color, pomp, or ceremony. Those lucky enough to be inside St. Peter's Basilica were participants in the greatest ecclesiastical conclave of modern times. Those outside were excited and awed by the phalanx of clergy sweeping St. Peter's Square with their scarlet, purple, white, or black robes. If nothing else happened at the council, it swept Rome into fever-pitch excitement.

Pope John arrived on his chair, which still made him dizzy as it swayed with the movement of its bearers. At the great bronze doors of St. Peter's, he dismounted and walked the length of the nave, smiling as he blessed the crowd.

117

After the celebration of the mass of the Holy Spirit, Pope John rose to deliver his sermon. He said that it was imperative for the Church to bring herself up to date. While the Church "must never depart from the sacred patrimony of truth received from the Fathers," she must "ever look to the present, to new conditions and new forms of life introduced into the modern world, which have opened new avenues to the Catholic apostolate." It was plain that the pope expected change. He did not want the old doctrines discussed phrase by phrase. He said that doctrine "should be studied and expounded through the methods of research and through the literary forms of modern thought." He spoke again and again of the prophets of doom—those men who look forever backward and seldom face the facts of a changing world. He seemed to emphasize the pastoral facet of the Church rather than the doctrinal—that is to say, the concerned, loving action of the Church rather than the validity of her teaching.

As for Christian unity he said, "The entire Christian family has not yet fully attained the visible unity in truth" desired by Christ. He spoke of "the brotherly unity of all," not only Christians but non-Christian religions as well.

From the beginning the key word to the council was "*aggiornamento*." No delegate was far from its meaning of renewal and reform.

After the opening day the Pope did not return to St. Peter's until the last session in December. He watched

Pope John walking in the gardens of the summer palace

the remainder of the proceedings on closed-circuit television.

The first business session got underway on October 13, with Cardinal Tisserant presiding. Each working day was from 9 A.M. to noon. At the first session the body had sworn an oath of secrecy, just as the cardinals had in conclave. The one thousand reporters were barred from inside St. Peter's, and only after violent complaints were they given daily briefings by Vatican officials on what had transpired.

Latin was accepted as the official language because all the representatives had it in common. Pope John expected it to curtail the length of speeches but it did not. Some delegates were concerned that Protestant observers could not follow the Latin services, but many of them were Latin scholars of high esteem and those who were not were given aids. The first session covered debate in six areas: liturgy, revelation, unity of the Church, communication media, nature of the Church, and the Virgin Mary.

From the beginning the official observers were graciously accepted. Pope John greeted the observers personally and also in groups. He talked with them informally. One observer said, "Pope John is not setting himself up as someone above us. He is with us."

On one occasion the pope said to the observers, "As far as it concerns my humble person, I don't like to claim any special inspiration. I am content with the sound doctrine that everything comes from God. . . . My eyes ranged over the multitude [referring to the first session of the council] of sons and brothers and suddenly as they rested on your group, on each of you personally, I drew extraordinary comfort from your presence. I will not say more about that right now, but will simply record the fact. Blessed be God for each single day . . . yet if you could read my heart perhaps you would understand more than words can say."

During the sessions many of the speakers, after greeting the "reverend fathers," would add "and dear observers" or "honored observers."

The observer response must have pleased Pope John even though the Greek Orthodox churches refused to send observers, saying, "Unless our delegates sit as full members, it is *not* an ecumenical council." However, at the last minute the Russian Orthodox Church sent Archimandrite Vladimir Kutlyarev.

Christian unity was much in Pope John's dream for his council. Some of the "separated brethren" had been divided for one thousand years. He wanted them back in the fold. Perhaps he worried particularly about this as the discussions wore on. He was urgent and eager. He wanted the council to produce a giant step toward reunion.

The very fact of seeing the whole church together must have been exciting for the Catholic world.

At first the council hours were steeped in traditional Catholicism, but John's "fresh air" was felt very soon, when the election of sixteen members to each of the ten commissions was scheduled to occur and names were proposed. The ten commissions were to present drafts for those documents proposed for discussion. (The documents were called *schemata.*)

When election rules were given and the slate read, Cardinal Liénart of Lille shocked everyone by proposing that regional (or national) caucuses meet and offer names for candidates. This would establish a worldwide base. This switch in plans surprised everyone, and pleased only some. From this point on Pope John recognized the winds of change. It was obvious that many delegates came for reform and renewal rather than to rehash and readopt all the old traditions.

The first session adjourned after fifteen minutes and the stunned delegates made their way from St. Peter's to reconvene with proposed candidates in several days.

A French newspaper said that this fifteen-minute session set the tone for the whole council. It called the event "a curtain raiser" and labeled it as one of three "curtain raisers." The other two were Pope John's opening speech showing "courage to think" and the council's message, "courage to speak." Cardinal Liénart's proposal was "courage to act."

The opening topics of discussion were liturgy and revelation. The first took three weeks and the second ended in a draw, when Pope John, seeing a stalemate, recalled the entire schemata and assigned it to a commission.

John was intensely interested in the debate concerning liturgy. He realized his dream for Christian unity could succeed or fail over theological differences related to it. For this reason liberal Cardinal Bea from Rome had been chosen especially to lead the thinking in this area. He had worked closely with the Anglican representative from England.

Much of the discussion revolved around whether or not parts of the Mass could be said in the native language of the people or must remain in Latin. Cardinal Ottaviani, a conservative, with great determination defended Latin as the traditional language. He said it offered unity to all Catholicism. Liberal views held that the Mass is worship and every worshiper should understand what is being said.

It was hard for reporters to see the alignment of thinking in some categories for discussion, but they quickly assigned the title of arch-conservative to Cardinal Ottaviani and liberal to Cardinal Bea. Both were brilliant men with a profound knowledge of theology.

The speeches were numerous and feelings ran high. Eighty-four-year-old Patriarch Saigh of Antioch asserted his liberal view by making his speech in French. He said there was nothing sacred about Latin. None of the churches of the Eastern rite used it, neither had Christ nor any of his disciples, and for the first two hundred years the Church itself had not even used it.

His speech was followed by a traditionalist who said, "Everything has been ordained by tradition and now you want to change it all."

At one point Cardinal Ottaviani spoke longer than

his ten-minute limit—much longer. When the presiding officer felt that Ottaviani had overdone a good thing, he pulled out the microphone cord and everyone applauded.

One day Pope John himself made a change in the liturgy to show that it could be done. It was the first change in one thousand years. He added the name of Saint Joseph after that of Mary in the Mass. To some this may seem like a small act, but it proved a point not only to the voting council delegates but to traditionalists everywhere that change is possible.

The first section of the schemata on liturgy passed by a vote of 1,922 to 11, after three weeks of discussion. The most important change allowed area bishops to decide whether parts of the Mass could be said in local languages. Changes were made immediately in many areas. This allowed congregations to better understand the service and gave them more participation in the worship. Hymns were introduced for congregational use. The sermon was given more of a place in the service. All these may not seem significant to Protestant readers who are used to singing hymns and having the sermon as the focal point of the service. But the shock which some Catholic congregations felt would be as greatly felt by Protestant worshipers if hymn-singing was suddenly omitted and ministers repeated the same prayers Sunday after Sunday in a foreign language.

Following the changes in liturgy the next schemata concerned the sources of revelation. Again it was an issue between conservatives and liberals. Traditional Catholicism holds that there are two sources of revelation—Holy Writ and oral tradition (from the time of the Apostles). Protestants recognize only Scripture.

The schemata for this discussion had been drawn up by Cardinal Ottaviani and close associates who completely ignored the nontraditional viewpoint. They felt that the Bible should be read only with the help of a theologian. The more liberal view felt that it must be studied in the light of what modern scientific minds are able to discover. They thought that such study enlightened and clarified the whole church and its responsibilities in the world.

After long discussions, Cardinal Bea won over the council on the grounds that Pope John himself had said in his opening council address that doctrine must be studied "through the methods of research and the literary forms of modern thought."

On November 21, Pope John restored order by withdrawing the schemata on Revelation and sending it to a commission where Cardinals Bea and Ottaviani, as joint chairmen, could work on it.

One Protestant observer remarked at this point, "Now I see why it can be a good thing to have a pope!"

No other issues stirred the assemblage as much as the first two. There followed discussions on the communication media, the Oriental churches, and the nature of the church, but none brought about critical discussions.

More than any discussion, Vatican II was shaken by the sudden illness of Pope John. The startling announcement was made that Dr. Antonio Gasbarrini of Bologna would be appointed as John's personal physician. Until this time he had been cared for by a doctor in Rome when necessary. His closest associates could see that it seemed very important for Dr. Gasbarrini, a brilliant doctor, to take charge.

On November 25, 1962, Pope John celebrated his eighty-first birthday. Although feeling ill, he forced himself to carry out a long exhausting day. The next day the worried public was told that he had a cold.

Several days later he was up and around, and the news came that he would sit by the open window in his room and recite the Angelus over loudspeakers with those gathered in St. Peter's Square. The council adjourned to be present for the occasion.

The crowds were wild with delight that Pope John was well enough to come to the window. After the Angelus they shouted and called to him. The pope allowed it for awhile, and then said, "My sons, Divine Providence is with us. As you see, from one day to the next there is progress. Not downward, but slowly upward. Sickness then convalescence." Then spreading his arms wide he said, "The Church grouped together here in its full membership. *Ecce* (hail) its bishops! *Ecce* its priests! *Ecce* its Christian people! A whole family is present here—the family of Christ."

On December 7, the day before council adjournment, Pope John made a surprise visit to St. Peter's during one of the sessions. The crowd shouted in great joy as he took his place on the throne of Saint Peter.

The next day he went again and walked the entire length of the nave. Everyone was thrilled to see him climb the steps to the microphone, and they listened intently as he said:

This Council in its reality, is an act of faith in God, of obedience to His laws, of sincere endeavor to correlate with the plan of redemption according to which the Word was made flesh of the Virgin Mary. . . . Now that the Bishops of the five continents are returning to their beloved dioceses . . . we should like to dwell a little on what has been done so far, and, encouraged and enlighted by this, to map out the future. . . . The first session was like a slow and solemn introduction to the great work of the Council—a generous willingness to enter into the heart and substance of our Lord's plan. It was necessary for brothers, gathered together from afar around a common hearth, to make each other's closer acquaintance; it was necessary for them to look at each other squarely in order to understand what was in each other's hearts. They had need to describe their own experiences, reflecting the conditions of the apostolate under the most varied climates and circumstances, in order that there should be thoughtful and profitable interchange of views on pastoral matters. In such a vast gathering it is understandable that a few days were needed to arrive at an agreement on a matter on which, in all charity, there existed, with good reason, sharply divergent views. But even this has a providential place in the triumph of truth, for it has shown all the world the holy liberty that the sons of God enjoy in the Church. . . .

In this hour of heartfelt joy it is as if the heavens are opened above our heads and the splendor of the heavenly court shines out upon us, filling us with superhuman certainty and a supernatural spirit of faith, joy, and profound peace. . . . In this light we look forward to your return. . . ."

On December 8, 1962, the council adjourned. It was scheduled to reconvene in September. Perhaps no one but Pope John himself knew of the malignant tumor which would take his life before the second session got underway.

CHAPTER SEVENTEEN

END OF AN ERA

FOR THE NEXT few months Pope John lived with the knowledge of his impending death. Much of the time he was in pain. He was too old for surgery, but doctors did what they could and warned against overexertion. But all their warnings did not slow down the man who set about his tasks with renewed urgency. Since nothing could be done to cure his illness, he worked on with intensified dedication. God guided his efforts, it seems, as the council had given the world a new face on Christian unity.

After signing his *Pacem in Terris* on April 12, 1963, he felt as though God alone had granted him a reprieve in time to carry on his work. But in late May, Pope John had another painful attack.

People all over the world grew alarmed. They prayed and held special services for his recovery. Then, as if by miracle, on Thursday, May 30, 1963, he seemed to get well. In fact, he seemed so much better that Doctor Gasbarrini announced, "It is conceivable that the pope may be able to bless the Sunday crowds in the square from his window."

But on Friday, May 31, the Pope cried out in terrible pain. Those around him were terrified. Pope John called his dear friend Capovilla, who was saying mass in the next room, and asked for the last sacrament.

"I am returning to the Lord. I offer myself as a sacrifice on the altar, for the Church, for the Council and for peace." To Doctor Gasbarrini he said, "My bags are packed and I am ready, very ready, to go." At this time he asked Capovilla to send for his brothers and sister, but he fell into a coma before they arrived.

The world continued to watch through the last hours of this marvelous man. They continued to pray that God, in the last minute, would perform a miracle.

Early Saturday morning it seemed for a moment that God had done just that. Pope John rallied and recognized his brothers and sister. He blessed them, talked quietly of old times and recalled all those who had been so dear to him throughout his long life. Then he fell unconscious. Those around him thought it would be his last moments before death, but all day Saturday he alternated between consciousness and unconsciousness. When he was conscious he knew everyone in the room. He spoke about his parents and the seminary in Bergamo.

Sunday was Pentecost, the seventh Sunday after Easter, which commemorates the day when the disciples of Jesus felt his presence again, after weeks of despair over his crucifixion. No one had expected the

Pope John shortly before his death in 1963

pope to live through the night. But he heard mass being said in the next room and asked that the Scripture concerning Pentecost be read again. He followed every word. Sunday was spent with people coming and going in his room until late afternoon. His family sat close beside the bed.

Pope John's confessor, Bishop Alfredo Cavagna, read his breviary, while Capovilla knelt praying in a corner. Pope John opened his eyes and called Capovilla to him saying, "When this is all over, be sure to go and see your mother." Capovilla wept.

Monday he was still alive. It had been a long weekend across the world as the faithful watched and prayed for their beloved leader. It is said that seventy-five thousand people stood in St. Peter's Square waiting for a sign of hope.

At 7 P.M. June 3, 1963, the pro-vicar-general of Rome celebrated mass for people in the square. Those inside Pope John's bedroom recited the rosary together. As the mass ended and the choir sang, Pope John died. The waiting was over. The world began its mourning.

By tradition, certain prayers are said over the dead body of a pope. After the officiating physician authenticates death, the pope is tapped three times on the forehead with a silver mallet, and is declared officially dead.

Change was not only Pope John's intention in life but in death as well. He had ordered simple ceremonies rather than the elaborate and traditional ones.

This description is from the carefully detailed biography of Pope John by Alden Hatch:

On Tuesday his body, clothed in white Papal vestments, lay in a simple bier in his apartment while those cardinals who were in Rome, the diplomatic corps, high officials, and his closest friends filed by. At six o'clock his body was carried in state down the royal stairway and across the square to St. Peter's. From eight o'clock Wednesday morning until six o'clock Thursday evening the sad crowds filed through the great basilica, where the council hall, with its banks of empty seats, still awaited the reconvening of the Ecumenical Council. High Requiem Mass was celebrated while the long lines of devout weeping people, John's people, moved slowly by. At six o'clock the doors were closed and half an hour later the body of the good Pope John was solemnly interred in the crypt beneath the High Altar. Later, it would be removed to the Basilica of St. John Lateran, where the Pope had wished to rest.

Prayers of the faithful from every religion followed him in death as they had in his few last months of life. His death also seemed to flow in the direction of brotherhood. Everywhere people mourned, but with their mourning they felt a quickened pulse toward Christian unity.

In the New Testament, the Gospel of Saint John, there is reported in Chapter 1, Verses 6–8 words which for many people offer summation to the life of Pope John XXIII, "There was a man sent from God, whose name was John. He came for witness, to witness concerning the light, that all might believe through him. He was not the light, but was to witness concerning the light."

Chronology

1881   Born in Sotto il Monte, Italy, November 25.

1892   Decides to become a priest. Enters seminary at Bergamo.

1904   Ordained a priest in Church of Santa Maria in Monte Santo, August 10.

1905–14 Secretary to bishop of Bergamo. Teaches classes at Bergamo Seminary and organizes Catholic Action groups.

1914   Drafted into Italian army as sergeant in medical corps. Later, as lieutenant, becomes hospital chaplain.

1921   Called to Rome by Pope Benedict XV to reorganize the Society for the Propagation of the Faith.

1925   Joins Vatican diplomatic service. Is given title of archbishop of Aeropolis. Appointed apostolic visitor to Bulgaria.

1935   Given title of archbishop of Mesembria. Becomes apostolic delegate to Turkey and Greece.

1936–52 Publishes five-volume history of Saint Charles Borromeo.

1944 Appointed papal nuncio to France by Pope Pius XII, December.

1952 Becomes Vatican observer to UNESCO.

1953 Made a cardinal by Pope Pius XII. Receives Legion of Honor from President Vincent Auriol of France. Appointed patriarch of Venice.

1954 Assigned as papel legate to Marian Congress in Lebanon.

1958 Becomes papal delegate to Lourdes, France, centenary. Pope Pius XII dies, October 9. Cardinal Roncalli elected pope on twelfth ballot, October 28. Crowned pope in five-hour ceremony at St. Peter's in Rome, November 4. Creates twenty-three new cardinals.

1959 Announces Vatican Council, January 25. Issues encyclicals on priestly perfection, Catholic missions, and the Holy Rosary. Issues *Ad Petri Cathedram,* referring to non-Catholics as sons and brothers.

1960 Invites archbishop of Canterbury to the Vatican as symbolic move of common intention to end prejudices. Asks forty non-Catholic observers to Vatican Council.

1961 Issues two encyclicals—*Mater et Magistra* on international social problems and commemorating Pope Saint Leo.

1962 First Ecumenical Council in Rome, October 11. Receives congratulations from Premier Khru-

shchev of the Soviet Union, November 25.
Issues encyclical on applying merits for success of Vatican Council II.

1963 Issues encyclical *Pacem in Terris* to all men
of goodwill—on international dignity of man,
equal rights of men and women, race equality,
disarmament, importance of the world community. Announces permission to celebrate
mass in vernacular of a country and gives permission for publishing Teilhard de Chardin.
Dies, June 3.

Bibliography

Ardi, Zsolt, James I. Tucek, and James C. O'Neill. *Pope John XXIII, An Authoritative Biography*. New York: Farrar, Straus, 1959.

Balducci, Ernesto. *John, the Transitional Pope*. New York: McGraw-Hill, 1964.

Berkouwer, G. C. *The Second Vatican Council and the New Catholicism*. Grand Rapids, Mich.: William B. Eerdmans, 1965.

Blanshard, Paul. *Paul Blanshard on Vatican II*. Boston: Beacon Press, 1966.

Brown, Robert McAfee. *Observer in Rome*. Garden City, N.Y.: Doubleday, 1964.

Daniel-Rops, Henri. *The Second Vatican Council*. New York: Hawthorn, 1962.

Fesquet, Henri. *Wit and Wisdom of Good Pope John*. New York: P. J. Kenedy, 1964.

Hales, E. E. Y. *Pope John and His Revolution*. Garden City, N.Y.: Doubleday, 1966.

Hatch, Alden. *A Man Named John*. Garden City, N.Y.: Doubleday (Image Books), 1965.

Klinger, Kurt. *A Pope Laughs*. New York: Holt, Rinehart and Winston, 1964.

Ormesson, Wladimir d'. *The Papacy*. New York: Hawthorn, 1959.

Pope John XXIII. *Journal of a Soul*. New York: New American Library (Signet Books), 1965.

Reed, Edward, editor. *Pacem In Terris*. New York: Pocket Books, 1965.

INDEX